The Lives of the
Desert Fathers

Also by BENEDICTA WARD SLG
  Sayings of the Desert Fathers

The Lives
of the
Desert Fathers

THE HISTORIA MONACHORUM IN AEGYPTO

Translated by Norman Russell
Introduction by Benedicta Ward SLG

MOWBRAY: LONDON & OXFORD
CISTERCIAN PUBLICATIONS: USA

ISBN 0 264 66581 3 (MOWBRAY cased)
ISBN 0 264 66428 0 (MOWBRAY paper)
ISBN 0 87907 834 0 (CISTERCIAN cased)
ISBN 0 87907 934 7 (CISTERCIAN paper)

First published 1981
by A. R. Mowbray & Co. Ltd
Saint Thomas House
Becket Street, Oxford, OX1 1SJ
and
Cistercian Publications
W.M.U. Station
Kalamazoo, Michigan 49008
(Number 34, Cistercian Studies series)

British Library Cataloguing in Publication Data

The lives of the Desert Fathers.–
   (Cistercian studies series; no. 34).
   1. Fathers of the church – Biography
   I. Russell, Norman   II. Series
   270   BR1705

   ISBN 0–264–66581–3 hardback
   ISBN 0–264–66428–0 paperback

Text set in 11 on 12 pt Monotype Poliphilus

Dedicated to
THE MOST REVEREND METROPOLITAN
ANTHONY OF SOUROZH
and
PROFESSOR JOCELYN TOYNBEE

ACKNOWLEDGMENTS

The authors wish to acknowledge the help they have had from each other in the preparation of this book: it has been a joint enterprise in every part, and the product of discussion over several years. The translation of the Greek text is the work of Norman Russell and the introductory chapters are by Benedicta Ward. The notes and the translation of Rufinus have been shared between them. The map was drawn by Norman Russell, who also compiled the indexes.

Each wishes to apologize to the other for defects and at the same time to express gratitude for the work of the other. In dedicating this book to Metropolitan Anthony Bloom and Professor Jocelyn Toynbee, each acknowledges a debt beyond words for the encouragement they have received in discovering the *saecula sine fine ad requiescendum* of the desert tradition.

CONTENTS

ABBREVIATIONS

Acta SS	*Acta Sanctorum,* ed. the Bollandists, Antwerp and Brussels, 1643 ff., in progress.
ACW	*Ancient Christian Writers,* ed. J. Quasten and J. C. Plumpe, Westminster, Maryland and London.
Anal. Boll.	*Analecta Bollandiana,* Paris and Brussels, 1882 ff.
DACL	*Dictionnaire d'archéologie chrétienne et de liturgie,* ed. F. Cabrol and H. Leclercq, Paris, 1907–53.
DS	*Dictionnaire de spiritualité,* ed. M. Viller, F. Cavallera and J. de Guibert, Paris, 1937 ff., in progress.
HM	*Historia Monachorum in Aegypto,* ed. A.-J. Festugière, Brussels, 1961 and 1971.
HM (Fr.)	French translation by A.-J. Festugière, *Les moines d'Orient* IV/1, *Enquête sur les moines d'Égypte,* Brussels, 1964 and 1971.
Lausiac History	Palladius, *Lausiac History,* ed. C. Butler, *Texts and Studies* 6, Cambridge, 1898–1904.
Life of St Antony	Athanasius, *Vita S. Antonii, PG.* 26, cols 835–976; trans. R. Meyer, *ACW* 10, 1950.
LSJ	*A Greek-English Lexicon,* ed. H. Liddell, R. Scott and H. Jones, Oxford, 1977.
Milne	J. G. Milne, *Egypt under Roman Rule,* London, 1924.
OCA	*Orientalia Christiana Analecta,* Rome, 1923 ff.
PG	Migne, *Patrologiae cursus completus. Ser. graeco-latina,* Paris, 1857–66.
PGL	*A Patristic Greek Lexicon,* ed. G. W. H. Lampe, Oxford, 1961.
Philotheos	Theodoret, *Histoire des moines de Syrie, SC* 234, Paris, 1977.
PL	Migne, *Patrologiae cursus completus. Ser. latina,* Paris, 1844–55.
Pitra	*Juris Ecclesiastici Graecorum, Historia et Monumenta,* ed. J. B. Pitra, 2 vols, Rome, 1864.
Rufinus	Rufinus, *Historia Monachorum in Aegypto, PL.* 21, cols 387–462.
SC	*Sources chrétiennes,* Paris, 1942 ff.
Veilleux	A. Veilleux, *La Liturgie dans le cénobitisme pachômien au quatrième siècle, Studia Anselmiana* 57, Rome, 1968.
White	H. G. Evelyn White, *The Monasteries of the Wadi'n Natrun:* Part II, *The History of the Monasteries of Nitria and Scetis,* New York, 1932–3.

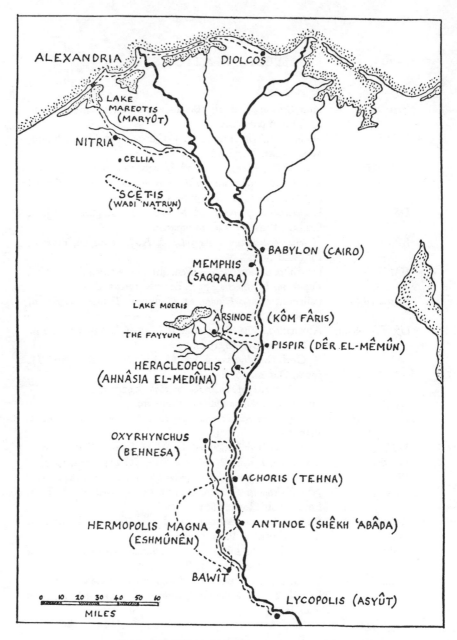

MAP OF THE JOURNEY INTO EGYPT

INTRODUCTION

CHAPTER I

THE *HISTORIA MONACHORUM IN AEGYPTO:*
TEXT AND SOURCES

'I hear that you are penetrating the hidden places of Egypt, visiting the bands of monks and going the round of heaven's family on earth . . . at last the full weight of truth has burst upon me: Rufinus is in Nitria and has reached the blessed Macarius.'[1] Thus Jerome in Antioch in 375 wrote to his friend Rufinus, and many years later Rufinus himself records this visit to Egypt with nostalgia: 'When we were drawing near this place they were aware that foreign brethren were approaching, and at once they poured out of their cells like a swarm of bees. With joyful speed and glad haste they ran to meet us;' and of the last stage of the journey to Scetis he wrote, 'This is the utter desert where each monk remains alone in his cell. . . . There is a huge silence and a great quiet there.'[2]

The 'huge silence', *silentium ingens, quies magna* of the desert was frequently invaded at the end of the fourth century by such visitors as Rufinus. Half a century earlier various monastic experiments had begun in the deserts of Egypt; they had flourished to such an extent that by 394 travellers reported that the population of the desert equalled that of the towns. *Anachoresis* was in the air and rumour of it spread throughout the Christian world. The central record of the early monks is to be found in the various collections of *Sayings of the Fathers*[3] which were compiled and circulated among the monks themselves. These anthologies of sayings attributed to the first monks of Egypt have a kind of authenticity which is unique. They are neither accounts of the way of life of the monks nor records of their teaching, but glimpses of them as they were known to their disciples; there is little literary artifice about such material: it is as rough and craggy as the landscape of Antinoë, 'that rugged desert in the mountain.' But these were followed by more sophisticated works. Antony the Great died in 356; within a year, Athanasius began to write an account of his life.[4] He had known Antony well, having spent some time with him as a young man, and Antony had visited him in Alexandria. The account was written in Greek and it was soon widely read in the Greek-speaking world; some years later Evagrius of Antioch translated the *Life* into Latin for 'the brethren from overseas' (*fratres peregrinos*) who were asking urgently for some account of the father of monasticism, because 'you have it in mind to model your lives after his life of zeal'. The *Life of St Antony* by Athanasius, and the Latin version by Evagrius,[5] is the first literary account of life in the deserts of Egypt in the fourth century. Its influence on monastic life and on hagiography was im﹍ mense.

In addition to this encomium of Antony the Great, however, there are various accounts written by the visitors who came to the desert during the fourth and fifth centuries. Travellers through Egypt had told of the monastic﹍ ism they saw there; the *Life of St Antony* confirmed their wonder; and fired with enthusiasm visitors began to undertake the journey into Egypt in order to learn from the monks at first hand; Basil the Great came, then Rufinus, Melania, Jerome, Palladius, and John Cassian with Germanus. It is from their accounts that a picture of life in the desert can be formed. It is a picture seen, of course, by outsiders, dependent on what they observed during brief visits and on what they were told. Moreover, these accounts are meant for the edification of a very different audience from the Coptic monks; they were primarily for the monks of the West, eager to follow the same spiritual path though under new physical and mental conditions. When visitors such as these came to Egypt they were received by the monks; they observed the life of the fathers and also shared in their conversations. There were others, however, the tourists of the desert, and with these the monks were more elusive: polite, but definitely not at home. One monk, for instance, had instructed his servant, with the diplomacy of the East, to distinguish when announcing two kinds of visitors; if he said to the old man, 'There are visitors here from Jerusalem,' he would welcome them and talk with them for as long as they wished to stay; but if the servant said, 'There are visitors from Egypt,' they would be given some food and sent away.

One of the journeys through Egypt at the end of the fourth century pro﹍ duced the account in Greek called the *Historia Monachorum in Aegypto*,[6] which has been translated here (pp. 49﹍119) and which I have chosen as the basis of this account of Egyptian monastic life. Despite the doubts of some modern scholars,[7] I am confident that the *Historia Monachorum* describes a real journey. Eighty years ago Dom Cuthbert Butler came to the same con﹍ clusion, and his chief reasons for doing so are still compelling. They are (1) that the eleven certain and two conjectural fixed localities follow, with the exception of Oxyrhynchus, an accurate south to north geographical order, which would have been impossible for anyone who had not been over the ground; (2) that the approximate ages of the chief solitaries are accurate for

394–5, the date of the journey; (3) that the dangers enumerated in the Epilogue have a circumstantial freshness about them.[8]

One problem for Butler was the odd position of Oxyrhynchus in the list of chapters, well attested in both the Greek and Latin versions, which appears to place this city too far to the south. If the author is describing a real journey, however, the position of Oxyrhynchus can be accounted for. The towns on the left bank of the Nile lie some way from the river. About forty miles below Lycopolis the Nile branches to the left. This subsidiary water-way, the Bahr Yûsuf, runs parallel to the Nile, passing Hermopolis Magna, Oxyrhynchus and Heracleopolis before flowing into Lake Moeris in the Fayyum. The travellers would appear to have descended the valley by the Bahr Yûsuf for the first part of their journey. The named places are therefore in an intelligible order and enable the journey to be reconstructed in some detail with plausible opportunities for the adventures mentioned in the Epilogue.

After visiting John at Lycopolis (Asyût) (i 1), the party sailed down the Nile until they came to the Bahr Yûsuf, which brought them to Ammon's monastery near Hermopolis Magna (Eshmûnen) (iii 1).[9] At some point en route they stopped to see Abba Or. From Hermopolis they continued down the Bahr Yûsuf to Oxyrhynchus (Behnesa) (v 1), calling on Abba Bes on the way. Not far from Oxyrhynchus they saw Theon. Then they cut across country back to the Nile, at this point ten miles to the east. Their experiences in the marshy ground and the swamp (Epil. 5–6) could have occurred at this stage. On reaching the Nile they sailed back upstream to Antinoë (Shêkh ʿAbâda), passing by Achoris (Tehna) without stopping. From Antinoë they made an expedition to see Elias (vii 1).

At this point the party split up. Perhaps the journey into 'the terrible desert' to see Elias has been too much for some of the brethren. The author with only two companions (viii 48) set out for Apollo's monastery at Bawit (viii 1),[10] another twenty five miles back up the Nile and then five miles or so to the west of the river. After a week with Apollo they set off into the desert with guides to see other fathers. Almost by chance they met Copres, who must have detained them with his stories for nearly as long as Apollo had done with his spiritual discourses. Finally they arrived at Achoris (Tehna) (xiii 1), which lies forty five miles north of Bawit in a direct line. It may be at this stage that, dispensing with guides after seeing Copres, they lost their way and spent their five days and nights in the desert (Epil. 4). At Achoris, where they saw Apelles, they may have rejoined the other members of the party, who had sensibly taken the easy route down the Nile from Antinoë.

From Achoris the party continued a further seventy miles down the Nile to Heracleopolis (Akhnasia el-Medina) (xiv 1) to visit Paphnutius's retreat. They then walked or sailed another twenty miles or so downstream to Pispir (Der el-Memun)[11] (xv 1), where they listened to Pityrion on the discernment of spirits. From Pispir they made their way overland to Arsinoë (Kôm Fâris) (xviii 1), which lies twenty five miles west of Pispir in the Fayyum. The wading through water for three days is likely to have happened at this stage (Epil.7). The next places to be mentioned are Babylon (near Cairo) and Memphis (Saqqara) (xviii 3). The direct route from Arsinoë lies forty five miles north-east across the desert. If the party took this route they could well have got lost (Epil.4). But perhaps they went back to the river, expecially if they had already learnt their lesson about desert travel.

Babylon and Memphis mark the beginning of the delta. The party continued their journey by water, taking the left branch of the Nile and then the canal known as the Lycus,[12] before disembarking near the village of Nitria (El Barnugi) (xx 5). It was on their way to Nitria that they encountered the crocodiles (Epil.11). While the party was in this area the author seems to have made a journey on his own to the Cells (xx 9). From Nitria the travellers crossed Lake Mareotis (Epil.10) and no doubt visited Alexandria, which lies on the opposite shore. On leaving Alexandria they made their way along the shore to Diolcos (xxvi), meeting with robbers en route (Epil.8). From there they probably took ship for a Palestinian port.

The places mentioned in the narrative fit in so well in the order in which they occur with the topography of Egypt that it is difficult to believe that the author's journey was a literary convention.[13]

The Latin text of the *Historia Monachorum* has always been regarded as the work of Rufinus of Aquileia. Jerome thought it was an original work by Rufinus though that was not the case. It is apparent from internal evidence that Rufinus did not make the journey described, though he had visited those parts of Egypt earlier and mentions several of the monks elsewhere in his writings. The *Historia Monachorum* in Latin is well known and is printed in *Patrologia Latina,* volume 21, cols 387–462. The Greek text is very similar to the Latin account and is earlier than the work of Rufinus. It seems probable that Rufinus used this as the basis of his account of Egypt, though with the additions and alterations appropriate to a man who had seen the places and people for himself and regarded the experience as the most treasured of his life. The Greek text was once thought to be part of the *Lausiac History* of Palladius,[14] but it has been shown to be an independent account through Butler's work. Père A.-J. Festugière has recently edited the text of the

Historia Monachorum as a separate work, which, despite some criticisms, remains the definitive version and is the text translated here. The author of the Greek work remains anonymous; Butler tentatively suggested Timotheus, archdeacon of Alexandria c. 412, as 'the merest conjecture to which I attach no importance';[15] Fr Derwas Chitty repeats Sozomen's suggestion with perhaps more weight than Dom Butler lent to the matter.[16] It seems, however, vain speculation to go beyond the fact that the Greek text claims to have been written by a monk from the monastery at Jerusalem on the Mount of Olives which was founded by Rufinus. He says he is describing a journey actually undertaken by himself and a party of six other monks from Palestine. The author's personality shows in at least two places where he uses the first person singular instead of the usual first person plural: that is, when he consults Apollo privately about the details of ancient Egyptian pagan religion, and when he goes by himself to inspect 'Joseph's granaries'— according to Rufinus, the pyramids. He also makes a separate expedition alone to see Ammonius, at a place perhaps to be identified as Cellia, or the Cells. Of an independent and inquiring mind, he seems to have been the guiding spirit behind the expedition as well as its recorder later.

The Latin version by Rufinus draws on his visit to Nitria in 375. Butler has discussed its relationship to the Greek text and also to the much shorter Greek version by Sozomen, which he concludes was an abbreviation of the Latin.[17] At the end of chapter xxix in the Latin version (cf. p. 154) Rufinus refers to the eleventh book of his own *Ecclesiastical History* for further information about Macarius, which was not written before 400. Since Rufinus died in 410, the account can be dated within ten years. As Butler has shown, certain passages in the Latin were added after Rufinus, notably the antiphon for the feast of St Cecilia, which is used in the first part of chapter I (John of Lycopolis), and the homily on the will of Christ attached to the name of Paul the Simple, but with its roots in the *Rule of St Benedict*. In the Latin version of Rufinus, however, the differences from the Greek are generally in accord with his manner of translation, which is to paraphrase and to introduce material which expands or clarifies the text. Like Evagrius with his Latin version of the *Life of St Antony*, Rufinus did not consider himself bound by a word for word rendering of the Greek: 'direct word for word translation from one language to another darkens the sense and strangles it,'[18] which in this case proves an acceptable procedure in fact if not in theory. The additions in particular of Rufinus are of value in themselves, and while they are distinguished from the Greek by a more polished style and literary sense, they contain insights otherwise lacking. The main additions, where they add to the text, have therefore been translated here. Particularly valuable is Rufinus's extra material on Nitria and Scetis, which is the main source for the topography of these monastic sites.

Let us now return to the experiences recorded in 394. It was not an easy journey into Egypt, and when John of Lycopolis congratulated the travellers with ponderous amusement on their determination to visit the desert there is a note of real admiration behind it:

> And what remarkable thing did you expect to find, my dearest children, that you have undertaken such a long journey with so much labour in your desire to visit some poor simple men who possess nothing worth seeing or admiring? . . . I marvel at your zeal, how taking no account of so many dangers you have come to us to be edified, while we from laziness do not even wish to come out of our cave.

They had come, they said, in order to learn about monastic life from the Egyptian monks, and they were to do so partly by conversation but even more by observation.

> We have come to you from Jerusalem for the good of our souls, so that what we have heard with our ears we may perceive with our eyes—for the ears are naturally less reliable than the eyes—and because very often forgetfulness follows what we hear, whereas the memory of what we have seen is not easily erased but remains imprinted on our minds like a picture.

The visitors were there both to observe and to listen. There seems to have been, surprisingly, no language problem in communicating with the monks. The party was composed of monks from Palestine from the Mount of Olives who spoke Greek and also Latin, but not, it seems, Coptic; they needed interpreters at several points where the old men knew no Greek. Among themselves it seems they spoke Latin, but mostly they were able to find someone who could understand Greek. The cosmopolitan state of community life in the desert is emphasised by the ease with which they managed to communicate. They found there men speaking a language they knew, as well as the Egyptian dialects. This had been the case from the beginning in Egypt when the monks had been joined by such men as the Roman Arsenius, an official in the palace of Theodosius.[19] Thus the way was opened for the visitors to hear and understand the teaching of the monks.

On the other hand, the monks themselves required a certain honesty among the visitors. When the party arrived at Lycopolis, one of the monks from Palestine who was a deacon seems to have disguised the fact in a slightly shame-faced manner as if he expected that lay life would be the norm for the monks they were visiting. John of Lycopolis immediately rebuked him for this innocent deceit:

> Do not spurn the grace of God, my child, and do not lie by denying the gift of Christ. For a lie is something alien regardless of whether its matter is grave or light.

It was a kind of tour undertaken by others. Jerome's friend and enemy Rufinus, as has already been said, visited Egypt in the company of Melania,[20] a young, wealthy and pious Roman widow who was escorted to Nitria by Isidore, a monk of Nitria and bishop of Damanhur. Melania spent six months there and visited several of the hermits, among them Pambo and Macarius the Alexandrian. She went back with Isidore to Palestine when the death of Athanasius placed an Arian on the episcopal throne in Alex-andria and many of the monks fled from Egypt. Rufinus stayed longer, for six years, at first as a disciple of Didymus the Blind. Finally he also went to Palestine and set up a community for men on the Mount of Olives, near the convent for women established by Melania.

Another visitor to Egypt was Evagrius, famous as a disciple of Origen and for his own mystical and ascetical writings. In 382 Evagrius came under the influence of Melania, when he fled from an unfortunate love affair in Constantinople. After six months of illness under the care of Melania on the Mount of Olives he decided that he would become a monk and, cured, he did so. He went to Nitria for two years and then on to the Cells, where he became one of the greatest of the monks.

In 385 Jerome himself came to Egypt through Palestine from Syria, where he met and joined company with the Roman lady Paula and her daughter Eustochium.[21] They stayed at Nitria and visited the old men before settling in Bethlehem in the following year. By that time the bitter quarrel between himself and Rufinus had disillusioned the admirers of this great example of antique *amicitia*.

Three years later Palladius came to Egypt and was received by Isidore, the friend of Melania, who made him a disciple of Dorotheus near Alex-andria.[22] After a brief period under the extreme rigour of this old ascetic. Palladius's health broke down and he returned to Alexandria. Later he set out again for Nitria and after a year there he went to the Cells and finally stayed with Evagrius as his disciple and friend until the death of Evagrius in 399. Never ready to stay in one place, Palladius paid many visits to the ascetics during this time, including one to John of Lycopolis, whose in-sight proved devastatingly accurate. Palladius wrote an account of the monks he had met for the benefit of Lausus, and this forms a companion document to the *Historia Monachorum*.

Finally, the most famous of the tourists of Egypt were John Cassian and his friend Germanus. They came from a monastery in Bethlehem where they had met Pinufius, a famous Egyptian monk who had anonymously shared their cell there for a time. About the year 385 they set out for Egypt, the home of sanctity. They returned about the year 400, having gone home only for a brief visit in the interval. Their experiences in Egypt formed the basis for Cassian's *Institutes* and *Conferences*[23] which were written in Latin between 420 and 430 for a monastery in Marseilles. These works circulated widely and were eagerly absorbed among the monks of the West, but the *Institutes* and *Conferences* are not verbatim accounts of conversations with the monks of Egypt; they are a carefully constructed interpretation of the aims and methods of monastic Egypt for the use of the monks of the West, and they are also shaped by the theological and ethical ideas of John Cassian. While they remain an authoritative presentation of the early ascetic life in Egypt which Cassian knew at first hand, their aim was to show men how to understand that life and adapt it to different conditions.

After the primitive sources of the *Sayings of the Desert Fathers* and before the sophisticated reinterpretation of Cassian took over there is an intermed⁄ iate stage, the travellers' accounts, in which the actions and words of the monks were seen and recorded by those who were eager to imitate them. These accounts also contained stories which were told and passed around as oral tradition in the desert besides what the visitors themselves had seen. This is what exists in the *Historia Monachorum*. It is a text which contains much of interest in itself but it also needs to be placed beside other early monastic texts, and this has been indicated to some extent in what follows.

NOTES TO CHAPTER I

1. *Letters of Jerome*, translated by T. C. Lawler, *ACW*, London, 1963, Letter 3, p 31.

2. Rufinus, *Historia Monachorum in Aegypto*, PL 21, 443C, 444C.

3. *Apophthegmata Patrum, Alphabetical Collection*, PG 65, 71–440. English trans⁄ lation by Benedicta Ward, *The Sayings of the Desert Fathers*, London & Oxford, 1975.

4. Athanasius, *Vita S. Antonii*, PG 26, 835–976. English translation by R. T. Meyer, *The Life of Saint Antony*, *ACW*, London, 1950.

5. Evagrius, *Vita S. Antonii*, PG 26, 833–976.

6. *Historia Monachorum in Aegypto*, Greek text ed. A.-J. Festugière, *Subsidia Hagiographica* 34, Brussels, 1961.

7. See, for example, Owen Chadwick, *John Cassian*, Cambridge, 1968, pp 7–8.

8. *Lausiac History*, vol. I, pp 198–203.

9. On the location of Ammon's monastery see p. 128, note III 2.

10. On the location of Apollo's monastery see p. 131, note VIII 5.

11. On identification of Pityrion's mountain see p. 134, note XV 1.

12. On the Lycus and Nitria see White, pp. 18–19.

13. The topographical section (notes 7–13) has been written by Norman Russell and may be used as a commentary on the map *(page x)*.

14. For a full discussion of these two texts see *Lausiac History*, vol. I, pp 10–15 and appendix 1, pp 276–7.

15. *Lausiac History*, vol. I, appendix 1, pp 276–7.

16. Derwas Chitty, *The Desert a City*, Oxford, 1966, p 51 and p 62, note 42.

17. *Lausiac History*, vol. I, appendix 1, pp 264–77.

18. Evagrius, *Vita S. Antonii*, epilogue, *PG* 26, 975B.

19. *Sayings of the Desert Fathers*, Arsenius 6; cf. Cyril of Scythopolis, *Vita Euthymii* c. XXI, trans. Festugière in *Les Moines d'Orient* III, 1–3, Paris, 1961–3.

20. *Lausiac History* c. XXXVIII.

21. Jerome, *Letter 108* to Eustochium; see J. Kelly, *Saint Jerome*, London, 1975, pp 278–9.

22. *Lausiac History* cc. I, II, LVIII.

23. John Cassian, *Institutes*, ed. and Fr. trans. J.-C. Guy, *SC* 109, Paris, 1965. *Conferences*, ed. and Fr. trans. E. Pichery, *SC* 42, 54, 64, Paris, 1955–9; English trans. Edgar Gibson, London, 1894, reissued by Erdmans 1973; new English translations are in preparation.

CHAPTER II

'THOSE BY WHOM THE WORLD IS KEPT IN BEING': THE SOCIAL ASPECTS OF THE TEXT

The first aspect of life in the desert which can be observed from the *Historia Monachorum* is that which is exterior to the monks themselves. There is information here about the place of the monks both in church and society in fourth-century Egypt. There are, first, the comments of outsiders on the role they have devised for the monks; and secondly there are indications of the ways in which the tensions of society influenced the preoccupations of the monks themselves.

To take the opinions of others about the monks first: the Prologue speaks at length about the monks as 'true servants of God . . . while dwelling on earth . . . they live as true citizens of heaven'; and later on the writer says, 'there is no town or village in Egypt and the Thebaid which is not surrounded by hermitages as if by walls. And the people depend on the prayers of these monks as if on God himself'; and finally he adds, 'it is clear to all who dwell there that through them the world is kept in being, and that through them too human life is preserved and honoured by God'. The monks are presented as the defenders, the guardians of the world's peace, constantly keeping watch on the frontiers, armed against the demons for the sake of mankind. It is a picture familiar enough in the Middle Ages; the three parts of society, those who fight, those who labour and those who pray, all working in their different ways for the life of the kingdom. Prayer was a great action to be fulfilled in the body politic; the monks were like trees, purifying the atmosphere by their presence.

This is a very explicit statement of a theme frequently discussed today, the place of the holy man in society.[1] The monk, especially the hermit, it is said, was, in fourth-century Egypt, a focus of spiritual power for his neighbours. As one who was outside society, disassociated from its petty factions and ambitions, he was a point of appeal, a peace-maker between men; he was also a friend of God, the one who had influence at the court of heaven; he was, at the very lowest, good luck for those fortunate enough to be near him. But this was the opinion of outsiders about the monk, not at all the opinion the monk had of himself. Occasionally, it was permitted, in the combat with the demons, for a monk to voice such an idea; Palladius, for instance, when he became restless and bored with life in the desert was told by Macarius, 'Tell them that for Christ's sake I am guarding the walls.'[2] But this is an exceptional comment in a specific situation. The monk sees himself, in this text as in others, as primarily the poor man, the sinner, the one who is defined, not by defence of others, but by his own need. It is, in fact, in this definition that the claim to 'keep the walls' finds its validity: the monk is 'involved with mankind' in the deepest sense, and where, by penʼ ance and prayer and selfʼloss, he learns to stand before God in a 'lifeʼtime's death in love', one part of torn and broken humanity is placed before its Saviour. When the monk defines himself, it is as a sinner, a weak man, not a strong one, not as one 'by whom the world is kept in being'.

It is with this in mind, that the opinion others have of the monks should be seen and discussed, and two aspects of this form the contents of the followʼ ing chapters: the opinion society had of the monks and the opinion formed by the visitors from Palestine. It must be emphasised that this is an external view and quite distinct from the monk's own aims and ideals: the idea of the monk as the one by whom 'human life is preserved and honoured by God' is, and must remain, an opinion from outside.

In the *Historia Monachorum* there are, first of all, alongside the definition of the monk in general terms as a champion for society in spiritual warfare, many indications of the very practical place the monk held in the life of fourthʼcentury Egypt. While one of the themes for the monks themselves was a radical withdrawal from society and its concerns, they inevitably created a new focus of order. In a visible as well as a spiritual way, the monks made the desert blossom. There are stories in the *Historia Monachorum* of flourishing agricultural projects—gardens of vegetables for the use of the monks and their visitors, green plants growing which were never there before, peasant farming in a rich soil, gardens for trees. Vegetables for cooking were taken from the garden of Copres for his visitors and these were the envy of his neighbours. Sarapion organized a regular trade between the Fayyum and the city of Alexandria on a large scale, sending wheat and clothing down to the poor of Alexandria; the reason given was that there were no poor near the monasteries:

> From the labours of the brethren they despatch whole shipʼloads of wheat and clothing to Alexandria for the poor, because it is rare for anyone in need to be found living near the monasteries.

Apollo may have been famous for his personal austerity and for fasting but when there was a famine in the Thebaid, the people assumed that Apollo's community of monks would have food and it seems in fact that they had plenty of baskets of bread which they shared with the surrounding district. The monks were naturally frugal, industrious and conscientious; it was the other side of their extreme poverty and asceticism.

The poverty of the monks provided moreover a means of communication, making them accessible to their neighbours. The contrast of rags and riches made its own impact. There is a story in the *Historia Monachorum* of the two old men called Macarius who went one day to cross the Nile; they boarded a ferry on which there were two tribunes:

> They had a chariot covered entirely in bronze, and horses with gold bridles, and a military escort, and servants apparelled in collars and gold cinctures. When the tribunes saw the monks sitting in the corner dressed in old rags, they blessed their simplicity of life. One of the tribunes said to them, 'Blessed *(Macarioi)* are you who have mocked the world'. Macarius of Alexandria said to him, 'We have mocked the world but the world mocks you. You should know that you have said this not of your own accord but by prophetic inspiration. For we are both called Macarius'. The tribune, moved to compunction by this remark, went home and took off his uniform, and after a generous distribution of alms chose to live as a monk.

This story shows another aspect of the place of the monks in society, in that the tribune had wealth to distribute before he became a monk. Again and again there are stories of converts who had wealth and either distributed it or took it with them into the desert. There was Melania, with her three hun׳dred pieces of silver which were so scorned by Pambo,[3] and in the *Historia Monachorum* Paphnutius met a converted bean and lentil merchant who had with him a vast amount of gold:

> He saw a merchant of Alexandria, a pious, Christ׳loving man, who dealt in business worth twenty thousand gold coins. He was making his way down׳stream from the Upper Thebaid with a hundred ships and dis׳tributing all his estate and his merchandise to the poor and the monks.[4]

Besides presents of this kind there are frequent stories of gifts of food to the monks whether of grapes, bread, or fruit.

Moreover, throughout the *Historia Monachorum* the Nile is apparent as the source of wealth. There are stories of the pagans taking their idols down to dip into the Nile to ensure flooding at the right time. There are equally stories of monks who were held to be responsible for the flooding of the Nile by their prayers:

John of Lycopolis was regarded by his fellow citizens as one who foreknew and revealed things hidden in the future; he told each man what
he had done in secret; and he predicted the rise and fall of the Nile and
the annual yield of the crops.

Copres seems to have been particularly involved in agricultural improvement in Egypt. While the visitors were talking to him, a peasant came in
with a shovelful of sand. The explanation Copres gave of this was as follows:

> The land bordering us was infertile, and the peasants who owned it
> scarcely had a double return from the seed they sowed. . . . I said to them,
> 'If you have faith in God even this desert sand will bear fruit for you'.
> Without a moment's hesitation they filled the folds of their tunics with
> the sand which had been trodden on by us, and bringing it to me, asked
> me to bless it. . . . They sowed the sand together with the corn in their
> fields and at once the land became extremely fertile more than anywhere
> else in Egypt. As a result, it is now their custom to do this, and every
> year they trouble us for sand.

The writer of the account adds that Copres himself took advantage of this
system of fertilization:

> He took us into his own garden and showed us date-palms and other
> fruit trees which he had planted himself in the desert. This had been
> suggested to him by the faith of those peasants to whom he had said that
> even the desert can bear fruit for those who have faith in God: 'For when
> I saw that they sowed sand and their land bore fruit,' he said, 'I tried to do
> the same and I succeeded.'

If the system is regarded as the transference of more fertile soil to other soil,
this is an instance of agricultural improvement of a high order.

The presence of gold in Egypt[5] is suggested in many places throughout
this account. Besides the tribunes with their golden bridles and golden
cinctures in the story of Macarius, Paphnutius mentions a robber who had
three hundred gold coins stored in his cave from which he payed arrears of
taxes for a woman he met in the desert. The merchant had a hundred ships
and twenty thousand gold coins. Patermuthius was once shown by the devil
'the treasure-vaults of Pharaoh full of pure gold'[6] and Theon was suspected
by robbers of hoarding gold in his cell.[7] There was then gold in Egypt and
the other side of this richness of the Nile delta lies in the references throughout the *Historia* to taxation. The first reference to monks in Roman law concerns the attempts of men to escape from their public duties of taxation and
military service by going off and claiming to be monks; they were to be
forced to return or have their property confiscated if they were not in fact

monks. This piece of legislation was said to have applied particularly to Egypt.[8] It was a rich land, ripe for taxation in money and in wheat.

The social dislocation which was the result of tax-avoidance is made clear in the *Historia Monachorum* in the story of Paphnutius, who met a robber in the desert who had helped a woman who was wandering there in extreme difficulty from just this burden of taxation. She told him:

> my husband has often been flogged during the last two years because of arrears of taxes amounting to three hundred gold coins. He has been put in prison and my beloved three children have been sold as slaves. As for me, I have become a fugitive and move from place to place. I now wander in the desert but I am frequently found and flogged. I have been in the desert now for three days without eating anything.

As well as flight from a burden of taxation there was in the desert the flight from the equal burden of military service. Conscription lay heavily upon Egypt as the frontiers of the Empire fragmented and more troops were needed. For a farmer to leave his holding which, in defiance of the vagaries of the Nile flood and the rivalry of his neighbours he had made into a viable concern, was a matter for anger and resentment; it was avoided when possible, and some of those who claimed to be monks were in fact objectors of an unconscientious kind. But the army was constantly present to the monks; some of them, like Pachomius himself, had been conscripts. Apollo heard that a monk had been conscripted 'in Julian's time' and went with some of his monks to encourage the man to endure; an astute garrison commander secured the whole group at least temporarily as forced conscripts, 'thinking they would make suitable recruits for the coming campaign'. Apollonius the monk and martyr seems to have been given a military guard when he was taken to Alexandria for trial. But even more significantly the images of military service were seared upon the subconscious of many of these men: they coloured even their dreams. Or told the visitors of a hermit, whom they realised was himself, who dreamed of demons as soldiers tempting him. He saw

> hosts of angels and a chariot of fire and a great escort of guards, as if an emperor was making a visit; and the emperor said, 'My good man, you have succeeded in every virtue; prostrate yourself before me and I will take you up like Elijah'.

But the monk was schooled in the basic virtue of the desert, the realism which is humility, and he said, 'I have Christ as my King whom I adore without ceasing; you are not my king' and the demons disappeared. In a very similar dream, Patermuthius drew different conclusions out of the same images:

He saw someone like an emperor who said to him, 'Do not keep watch, pondering on tombs and these petty crimes. If you wish, instead, to change your way of life to one of virtue, and to enter military service with the angels, you will receive the power to do so from me'.

As the writer says in the Prologue, the monks were enlisted in the king's army; they kept watch, on the alert, 'like an army expecting its emperor'.

The impression made on the minds of the monks by Roman taxation and conscription was great; but nearer to home was the paganism of the villages. The Christianity of Egypt was a new thing; the diocese of Alexandria was a flourishing Christian centre by the third century, but the sanctuaries of the ancient gods of Egypt remained along the Nile, and the *Historia Monachorum* is full of references to the pagans who surrounded the monks. Even in Alexandria, the situation was far from secure and in 391, three years before the seven came to Egypt, the issue had come to a head: the pagans had rioted and imprisoned Christians, and withstood siege in the temple of Sarapis, until it was razed to the ground by imperial command and the image of Sarapis was destroyed. An ominous story connected with this was told of the monks: 'Theophilus the archbishop summoned some fathers to go to Alexandria one day to pray and to destroy the heathen temples there'.[9] presumably an indication that the archbishop had discovered the strength of the monks and was harnessing it to the destruction which was to earn the monks the name of fanatics among civilized men.

On a local level both John of Lycopolis and Copres had dealings with the pagans and their farming projects, while Apollo spoke to the seven visitors at length about the paganism of Egypt.[10] He explained the polytheism still prevalent in an ingenious way, suggesting that there were practical reasons for deifying nature:

> They deified the ox . . . because by means of this animal they carried on their farming and produced their food. They deified the waters of the Nile because it irrigated the whole countryside . . . .

A modern anthropologist would say much the same. Apollo suggested with more ingenuity than probability that animals were deified because in attending to them the Egyptians were too busy to follow Pharoah in his pursuit of the Israelites and for that reason they escaped drowning and were correspondingly grateful to what had held them back.[11]

The writer of the account seems to have been personally fascinated by the pagans; he talked privately to Apollo about their beliefs and went off alone to see the pyramids when they reached Cairo. He gives some accounts also of the dealings of the old men with the pagans where the two cultures clashed.

The ceremonies necessary for the flooding of the Nile[12] were of central importance in Egypt, and, as has been said, John of Lycopolis was asked to
bless the waters in place of the pagan priest. Apollo met a procession of
pagans taking a statue to dip into the Nile waters, and caused commotion
among them and in the neighbouring villages by halting the procession by
his prayers. The conversion of these pagans followed, but this did not end
Apollo's dealings with others: he was asked to make peace in a pagan
village and spent considerable time catechising a brigand chief there,
who became both a Christian and a monk. Another such champion was
not so fortunate, and in a dispute over land with Christians he alone was
killed, thereby confirming his fellow villagers in respect for the Christians
and their powers. A story retold about Macarius attributes the illness of a
girl to 'magic arts' which are counteracted by the prayers of the saint. The
paganism of the Egyptian villages lay all around the monks; part of their
rejection of the villages was their rejection of the paganism interwoven into
life on the land; and the conversion of the pagans was, if not a major concern, at least something which they would do if they could. The pagan
temples were always there, and the monks used them as monasteries in
Oxyrhynchus. The pagans were their own recent past, to be forsaken and
left behind, not explored and reasoned with. Macarius once slept in a deserted
pagan temple at Terenuthis and dreamed of demons inhabiting the mum-
mies he found there; but it was the same Macarius who converted a pagan
priest by seeing him as a man to be treated with consideration rather than
as an enemy to be attacked.[13]

The monks had a place in the society of Egypt which is many sided, and
the *Historia Monachorum* provides glimpses of these men in their situation
among pagans, farmers, Romans, merchants, soldiers, civil servants and
their families, among the towns and villages, enclosed by the varied and
lusty life of the Nile delta. The air of another country, of the ages without
end, which surrounds the monks in their literature had some basis in fact;
their own aims were directed to a vast silence, a huge quiet, in the world
without end deserts; but they were nevertheless set in a society and came
from it, and it was a society which shaped their thoughts and ambitions as
well as their temptations, and a society which made a place for the monks
both as arbiters and, later, as the champions of its own orthodoxy.

NOTES TO CHAPTER II

1. See, for example, Peter Brown, 'The Rise and Function of the Holy Man in Late Antiquity', *Journal of Roman Studies* 61 (1971) pp. 80–101.

2. *Lausiac History* c. XVIII.

3. *Lausiac History* c.x: 'I spoke to him: "So you may know, O Lord, how much it is, there are three hundred pounds". He did not so much as raise his head, but said: "My child, He who measures the mountains knows better the amount of silver. If you were giving it to me, you spoke well; but if you are giving it to God, who did not overlook the two obols, then be quiet".'

4. The Roman *solidus*, called the *nomisma* in Egypt, was a gold coin created by Constantine; after the reform of coinage under Diocletian it replaced the drachma as the standard unit for Egyptian accounting. See A. H. M. Jones, *The Later Roman Empire 284–602*, Oxford, 1973, vol. i, pp. 107–8.

5. Egypt was the richest province of the Roman Empire and there is abundant surviving evidence of gold there; it was collected from among the deposits along the Nile or, later, mined from quartz rock, usually by criminals or soldiers. cf. R. H. Greaves and O. H. Little, 'Gold Resources of Egypt', *Report of the XVth International Geological Congress*, 1929, 123–7.

6. Museum collections of wealth found in the royal pyramids illustrate this; cf. Cyril Aldred, *Jewels of the Pharaohs*, London, 1971.

7. Cf. *HM* X, Patermuthius the robber was planning to rob the house of an anchoress, presumably under the impression that her second inner chamber contained wealth. This suspicion was often levelled at hermits; for a medieval example, see John of Ford, *Life of Wulfric of Haselbury*, ed. Maurice Bell (Somerset Record Society 47, 1932) c. 49, p. 115 and c. 43, p. 103.

8. *Theodosian Code* XII,18,1 (AD 368) and XII,1,63 (AD 373). The need for conscripts on the frontiers was increasing. Pachomius had been a conscript for Maximian's last war against Licinius. d. 313. Cf. *Sancti Pachomii, Vita Graeca A*, c. 4.

9. *Sayings of the Desert Fathers*, Theophilus the Archbishop 3; and Bessarion 4.

10. The suppression of pagan worship was ordered by law, *Theodosian Code* XVI,10,11; but its application must have varied according to local conditions.

11. The worship of pagan Egyptians connected with animals is frequently referred to in early Christian texts; the reference to the worship of vegetables I have been unable to find elsewhere.

12. The season for the flooding of the Nile was August to the end of November; crops could be grown in abundance in the deposit left by the waters provided they could survive the salt content; cf. W. Willcocks, *Egyptian Irrigation*, London, 1889, p. 20.

13. *Sayings of the Desert Fathers*, Macarius the Great 39.

CHAPTER III

THE MONASTIC PATTERN IN EGYPT

The party of seven were eager to learn and acute in observation, but it was not any social aspect of monasticism that interested them; rather it was the monastic life itself. Whatever could be seen of the life of the monks of Egypt, they saw, and, with some measure of naïvety, they recorded it. The overall impression from their account is of a diversity and a fluidity in life-styles, ranging from total enclosure in the walled monastery of Isidore to the wandering hermits like John. It is clearly the second generation in Egypt, where the lives of the great old men were already a legend, and where groups in monasteries were more usual than the isolated wandering hermit, but the sense of a variegated spiritual landscape remains. The visitors had come because they had read or heard about the spiritual athletes of Egypt and they took mental snapshots for the long evenings at home.

The numbers given in the *Historia Monachorum* are a cause for com-ment.[1] If all the numbers given for monks and for nuns in this small part of the world which was visited by the Palestinians were added together it would give a figure well in excess of the whole population. It is no longer enough to dismiss such numbers at once as fantastic and imaginary; a les-son of caution has been learned from archaeological finds which have con-firmed some of the claims which were once easily dismissed. It was after all a very popular way of life. And it is possible that these numbers included the saints of the monastery, that is, the dead in them. Whatever they may mean, the number of monks is always given in round figures: Or has 'ten myriads' of disciples, and a 'thousand' monks; Ammon has three thousand monks; in Oxyrhynchus there are ten thousand monks and twenty thousand nuns. All that can be counted on in this is that there were many monks and nuns to be seen in the places visited. Moreover other figures arouse suspicion when taken too literally: were all the great hermits nonagenarians when the visitors arrived? Or is this age of ninety simply an indication of the nearness of these old men to the full perfection of a hundred?

The most vivid impression made by this account of life in monastic Egypt is of the great variety of ways of life there. For instance, the monks were housed in several different ways: there was John of Lycopolis who lived in a two-roomed cell, with a window through which he saw those who visited him daily. He received the Palestinians personally and ate and talked with them inside the guest cell for several days after their arrival. They lived, however, with the other monks in a kind of small monastic village several miles away from his cell. On the journey they met other hermits who lived alone in caves which were plentiful in the district; there is a dramatic picture of the old man Elias, seated under an overhanging rock, trembling with age, alone in 'the terrible desert'; he had been there since before the memory of any of the rest of the monks. He had, it seems, nothing to say; they looked at him and they left; he seemed to them almost a relic of an earlier age.

The most usual way for the monks to live was in a small self-built cell constructed of bricks and mortar with one or possibly two rooms. These could be built in a day and the *Historia Monachorum* gives two instances of this. For example, Or organized his monks when they came to live near him:

> He called together everybody who lived near him and built cells for them in a single day, one delivering mortar, and another bricks, another drawing water, and another cutting wood. And when the cells had been completed, he himself saw to the needs of the newcomers.

Such team-work was apparently the custom also in Nitria and the writer gives a similar account of the building of cells there. Ammonius,[2] for instance, at Cellia, used to call his community together when new members arrived, and 'giving bricks to one, and water to another, completed the new cells in a single day'. Ammonius himself was said to have had a particularly beautiful cell with a courtyard and a well, making it self-sufficient and essentially private. The cells for hermits seem to have consisted of two rooms, an outer chamber and an inner one for sleeping: the anchoress who was visited by the robber Patermuthius had a cell with two rooms situated near a church run by monks who could look after her. John of Lycopolis had a two-roomed cell and built on another room in which to receive guests.

Besides these simple two-roomed cells, grouped loosely together, there were also monasteries, more permanent buildings for groups of monks in the district. The seven visited a monastery built on the pattern of the cenobitic community of St Pachomius at Tabennisi,[3] in which there was a single large building to house all the monks, with a common refectory and a church. There was also the monastery of Isidore in the Thebaid which seems to have had an especially strict view of the need for monks to remain within the walls of their monastery.

> The monastery, says the writer, 'was fortified with a high brick wall . . . Within the walls were wells and gardens and all that was necessary to

supply the needs of the monks, for none of them ever went out. The gate keeper was an elder, and he never allowed anyone to go out or to come in unless he wished to stay there for the rest of his life without ever leaving the enclosure'.

This goes beyond the concept of the monastery as necessarily fortified against the attacks of wandering nomads[4] and lays emphasis on the desire of the monks to remain undisturbed within the walls of the monastery. The monastery of Isidore seems to have been the one place where the visitors were not allowed to talk freely with the monks. The other instance of more permanent buildings is Oxyrhynchus, a town of the Thebaid which flourished in Christian Egypt and had its own bishop. The travellers saw it as filled entirely with a population of monks and nuns, who lived in the deserted temples and treated the town as a gigantic monastic establishment.

The monastic buildings seen by the seven travellers were of the simplest kind. The monks built with bricks made from mud and dried in the sun, and what was necessary to existence determined everything about the work. This restriction to essentials is a fundamental aspect of the life of the monks of Egypt. There is no mystique here of bare and simple buildings, but a necessary poverty dictated by the materials and time available. Manual work, similarly, was the work of the monks, not for any theory of the need for a balanced time-table but because he who did not work did not stay alive very long. The monks were intensely concerned to discover that freedom of heart that enables a man to see God and it was this that determined their austerities. They sought the frontiers of human experience in every way, including the places where they chose to live and the shelters they built there. The monks were involved in a great experiment with human nature in its relationship with God and this gave them an aim beyond the austerities themselves. On the one hand, there were the plain limitations imposed on them by life in a desert; on the other there was the use they chose to make of it.

In Egypt the visitors noticed the routine of the monks in their daily life, and commented on their practices about the basic things of life, food, sleep and clothing. First of all, they saw that the monks regulated and controlled the need for sleep. The writer in the Prologue says they 'kept watch waiting for Christ like loyal sons waiting for their father'. Some of the monks of Apollo at Bawit stayed awake all night: 'I saw them myself with my own eyes begin their hymns in the evening and not stop singing until the morning'. Anouph claimed to be one of the 'sleepless ones': 'I have not slept in the day nor have I ceased to seek God at night'. The hermit John began his ascetic life by standing under a rock 'for three years in uninterrupted prayer, not sitting at all or lying down to sleep, but simply snatching some sleep while standing'. The monks of Nitria also practised this extreme in keeping watch and the writer says of them, 'Some of them never slept at night, but either sitting or standing persevered in prayer until morning'. The attitude is positive; the monks are not refusing to sleep but 'keeping watch'; it is the implementation of the austere saying of Arsenius: 'one hour's sleep a night is enough for a monk if he is a fighter'.[5]

The same experiment with the limits of natural life was followed in various forms about food. There are instances in the *Historia Monachorum* of extremes in fasting: John the hermit, for instance, was said to have begun by going without food for three years except for Communion on Sundays. This story should be read with caution since it is part of a series of tall stories which Copres offers to the visitors in order to make his own ascetic achievements sound minor by comparison with others; however, it is of interest because even in this context the common sense of the desert in not going beyond what is possible for men is displayed: an angel rebukes John for his fast and suggests, with the irony so typical of these texts, that he has had enough of the rich food of fasting: 'this spiritual food is sufficient, otherwise your stomach will become heavy and you will vomit'. Some of the monks ate very little, like John of Lycopolis who ate only a little fruit each day and Pityrion who had a light diet of a little cornmeal soup each day. At Bawit it was customary to keep the canonical fasts of Wednesday and Friday, days of complete abstinence from food, in memory of the Passion of Christ, but on other days a meal in the evening, usually after Communion, was the norm. Older monks might eat very little simply because of age, but the custom observed by the travellers seems to have been that referred to in the *Sayings of the Desert Fathers* as usual in the desert after the first days of experiment:

> Abba Joseph asked Abba Poemen, 'How should one fast?' Abba Poemen said to him, 'For my part, I think it better that one should eat every day, but only a little, so as not to be satisfied'. Abba Joseph said to him, 'When you were younger, did you not fast two days at a time, abba?' The old man said, 'Yes, even for three and four and the whole week. The Fathers tried all this out as they were able and they found it preferable to eat every day, but just a small amount. They have left us this royal way, which is light.[6]

By the time Cassian came to Egypt, this custom seems to have become universal and the visitors from Palestine observed that this was already the case. They were given food when they arrived at a place, but usually the monks ate a light meal at the ninth hour of the day.

It was not only the frequency of eating that was restricted but also the kind

and quantity of food. In this also there is the same mixture of the limits imposed by the nature of life in the desert and the concern of the monks with the
essential matter of being free to feed on the word of God without distraction
by appetite. The quality of food in the desert was, of necessity, not noticeably
poorer than that of the average peasant; indeed it might be better. A comparison which delighted the monks was that between the sophisticated food
eaten by Arsenius at court and the poor fare he had in the desert; one story, in
various versions, contrasted this with the experience of the average peasant
turned monk: 'What was your food in the fields and what wine did you
drink?' 'I ate dry bread and, if I found any, green herbs and water.'⁷ This is
precisely the diet described in the *Historia Monachorum* for the hermits the
visitors encountered or heard of: dried bread and green herbs. The bread,
paxamatia, consisted of small loaves, about twelve ounces in weight, which
could be taken into the desert and stored indefinitely; it is this kind of bread
which was found in abundance at Bawit during a famine. To this, salt
might be added when the loaves were soaked again to make them edible and
only the most austere of hermits regarded that as a luxury.⁸ A hermit might
cultivate a small garden but any vegetables he grew would be for visitors. It
seems from this account that the vegetables were salted in brine to preserve
them for future use.

In the monasteries, some cooking was possible, and at Nitria the visitors
saw fresh bread. The Pachomian monks ate soup, as well as olives with
bread, as did the disciples of Helle. The merchant who gave away beans and
lentils to the monks at his conversion does not seem to have had his gift
rejected, while it was said of Apollo that he did not eat lentils, as if this were
unusual. Water was the usual drink and in this account that is all the visitors
were offered, though elsewhere in this literature wine is mentioned as not
being forbidden.⁹

The dry parched air of the desert, the amount of salt in food, the brackish
water, are all reflected in the visions and fantasies of the monks. What they
dream about is fresh, juicy fruit and from such dreams one obtains a very
clear if oblique light on the fasts of the hermits. What were their luxuries?
Grapes, which would be passed from hand to hand in wonder; figs, sometimes monstrous figs which were held to be the real fruits of paradise. Apollo
and his first disciples were given an exotic gift one Easter, from the hand of
an angel:

> Things which do not grow in Egypt: fruits of paradise of every kind,
> and grapes and pomegranates and figs and walnuts . . . and honey-
> combs, and a pitcher of fresh milk, and giant dates, and white loaves
> still warm.

The milk that is fresh, the bread that is warm, the honeycomb, only source of sugar for the ancient world, and above all the soft, delicious fruits. When Patermuthius and Macarius each dreamed themselves into paradise, the first thing they did was eat, and it was of fruit, 'rich and many-coloured' fruit; that was the real reward.

The monks disciplined themselves over sleep and food. Their clothing was also a matter of ascetic discipline. The visitors looked to see how the monks were dressed and this is described more than once. The early traditions of the desert show the hermits as wandering about in rags or the simplest of tunics. The hermit Paul was said to have woven himself a tunic out of palm-leaves.[10] In this account Macarius is said to be dressed in rags and Helle was dressed in 'a rag with so many patches' that it provoked a priest to gentle sarcasm. But the custom of wearing a distinctive dress was already well established and its details are described. One set of clothes was customary, and a story is told of a monk who tried to get more by hiding his first set. In the monasteries, formal dress is required: Apollo and his monks wear a tunic and a linen head-dress; the monks of the Pachomian mon-astery have their sheepskins and linen head-covering. In church the monks were said to be dressed in white, 'like the angelic choir'. There is above all a detailed description of the dress of a monk, which Copres says was invented by Patermuthius. He describes a short-sleeved tunic, a hood, a sheepskin cloak, a linen cloth round the waist, as the clothing he bestowed upon a young man who wished to be his disciple. This is comparable with the monastic dress described by John Cassian some years later[11]: there is the *colobium*, a short-sleeved tunic, the ordinary dress of a working man; the hood, or *cucullus*, which was used among the Tabennisiots; the *melote* or *mafort*, a sheepskin, which was used in various ways, most of all out of doors as a cloak; he mentions also the *planeta*, a girdle to keep the tunic out of the way at work. While too much should not be made of this story of Copres, it seems that the travellers were told of a distinctive dress used among the monks of Egypt, though no special significance is yet given to it.

The work of the monks was mostly agricultural of necessity. There was the daily fight for existence for those who chose to live away from the settled lands near the fertile Nile. They grew their own herbs and vegetables, and certain groups grew corn for bread. Some corn was apparently exported and the labour of the monks was used at harvest, for which they received the usual wage of a labourer, a picture confirmed in the *Sayings of the Desert Fathers*.[12] Flax was also grown, and the monastery of Sarapion had a flourishing trade in flax and wheat with Alexandria. Copres was interested in farming, both on his own behalf and for the peasants around him, and various fathers made the wilderness blossom by their efforts. There was some demand for other trades in the desert, and the hermit John wove harnesses for asses; Apelles in the district of Achoris continued as a monk to ply his trade as a blacksmith and made tools for the monks to use. There is very little mention of study or of the work of reading or copying books, an omis'sion which is probably not especially significant. Evagrius, the most learned of monks, talked to the visitors at Nitria and was clearly admired for his learning; moreover there is evidence elsewhere in these sources of a basic reverence for the study of the Scriptures. Even here, the knowledge of the Scriptures is mentioned as 'the highest degree of *ascesis*', when Patermuthius is able to read a book given him, in spite of having been illiterate for most of his life.

The monks chanted the psalms continually, and this basis of prayers and canticles is taken for granted by the visitors. What is more surprising in their account is the number of times they mention the celebration of the Eucharist and Communion. The impression given in other sources is that few of the monks of Egypt were priests and the daily celebration of the Eucharist was not central to their way of life. Even the regular saying of prayers at certain times each day was regarded as a dangerous innovation by some of the early fathers[13] and the celebration of the Eucharist was a luxury for towns'folk. Here, however, both hermits and monks in groups and in monasteries are said to have celebrated the Eucharist and received Commun'ion frequently. Copres, Eulogius, Isidore and Piammonas were all priests and John of Lycopolis begins his conversation with the visitors by a sharp reminder that ordination is not something to be disclaimed. Very often they described their welcome as being a greeting, the washing of feet, a Eucharist and a meal.[14] At Nitria the familiar pattern is described of a Saturday and Sunday Synaxis, attended by all the brothers: the monks 'come together in the churches only on Saturdays and Sundays . . . they do not see each other except at the *Synaxis*'. The hermit John received Communion each Sunday from a priest even in his most extremely ascetic day, and however much he wandered in the desert, each Sunday found him back there for this act. When Helle visited a monastery, he was amazed to find that they had no priest to celebrate the *Synaxis* on Sunday and immediately set about fetching one from a village across the river; it was not his fault that the priest was too timid to use the unorthodox means of transport Helle provided. Piammonas, Macarius, Dioscorus and Pityrion were all adept at discovering the attitude of mind with which others approached the sacrament and made it a matter of central importance that they should approach only with purity of mind. It is however at Bawit in the monastery of Apollo that the Eucharist is most fully described and in which it had a central position. The Eucharist was celebrated daily in Apollo's monastery and he told the visitors that

> Monks, if possible, should communicate daily in the Mysteries of Christ ... It is therefore useful for monks ... to be ready every day, and to pre-pare themselves in such a way as to be worthy to receive the heavenly Mysteries at any time, because it is thus that we are also granted the forgiveness of sins.

The picture of a monastery of five hundred monks and hermits with a daily celebration of the Coptic Liturgy at the ninth hour and with a night vigil is unusual in these sources: the recognised pattern for the Egyptian monks was that described by Cassian, when the monks met on Saturday and Sunday for the purpose of receiving Communion.[15] This is the custom described by the *Historia Monachorum* at Nitria. Rufinus adds a few details to the picture of the Eucharistic celebration in his story of the demons who tempted the monks at the Liturgy: the altar was in full view, the monks stood to pray, making prostrations, and they received Communion in their hands. It is possible that the visitors from Palestine were selective in their record, and since they were welcomed so often to the Eucharist when they visited the monks, their account gives a greater predominance to it than was normally the case; it may also be that they were particularly interested in any custom which was similar to the customs of their own monastery. But this is speculation and the fact remains that the visitors from Palestine record more liturgical activity than any other source for the Egyptian monks of the fourth century.

The monastic life as observed by the visitors supplements the picture that can be built up from the *Lausiac History*, the *Sayings*, Cassian and other sources. The Palestinians were eager to observe and took care to listen to whatever was told them, accepting much that may have been embroidery rather than fact. They do not however suggest that the more extreme ascetic practices are to be imitated by their readers: the signs and wonders of the monks are to be admired, it is their virtues that are to be imitated. The inner world of detachment from self and freedom of heart towards God is central: 'Let this be a sign to you of progress in the virtues when you have acquired mastery over the passions and the appetites. For these are the beginnings of the charisms of God'.

NOTES TO CHAPTER III

1. Cf. Paul Devos, 'Les nombres dans l'Historia Monachorum in Aegypto', *Anal. Boll.* 92 (1974) pp. 97–108.
2. Ammonius was at Cellia, about twelve miles distant from the main group at Nitria (see map).

3. There were two monasteries of Tabennisiots near Hermopolis Magna, of which this was one.

4. Cf. The White Monastery, *monasterium candidum*, near Atripe, where the walls were blank, with two tunnels only for entrance.

5. *Sayings of the Desert Fathers*, Arsenius 15.

6. Ibid. Poemen 31.

7. Ibid. An Abba of Rome 1.

8. Ibid. Achilles 3. Cf. *Life of St Antony*, 7: 'his food was bread and salt, his drink water only.'

9. Ibid. Sisoes 8.

10. Jerome, *Vita S Pauli*, trans. Helen Waddell, *The Desert Fathers*, London, 1936, p. 52. It was worn by Antony the Great in memory of the other hermit.

11. *Institutes* I, 5ff.

12. *Sayings of the Desert Fathers*, Benjamin 1; Isaiah 5; Pior 1.

13. Ibid. Epiphanius 3.

14. Note that this was the customary greeting of guests in Christian Egypt, though the addition of a Eucharist in place of prayers was unusual. Cf. *HM* XIV for Paphnutius and the head-man of the village.

15. *Institutes* III 2; *Conferences* III.

CHAPTER IV

THE SINGLE EYE: THE IDEALS AND INSIGHTS OF MONASTIC EGYPT

The monks of the Egyptian desert could be observed and their outward conduct recorded; but the visitors had other interests. They were concerned to learn from the old men the inner meaning of monastic life, and in the record they made later of the journey, there is a good deal of material about desert ideas and ideals as the monks themselves understood them. In the first and longest chapter, the writer describes their visit to John of Lycopolis, one of the most famous of the desert fathers, whose existence and exploits are known from other sources also. The passage is long and it is complete in itself, ending with a doxology. It is a carefully constructed piece of literature, designed to convey an impression, rather than a simple narration of facts. It contains in itself the essential teaching of the desert as it was understood by the writer.

What does the writer make John of Lycopolis, the adviser of princes, say to his visitors? He greets them with the traditional courtesy of the desert, and they settle down for conversation. The scene in a small cell on a distant hill-side is no doubt a literary reminiscence, combining two or more such visits in a whole. The visitors, as was customary, asked him to speak to them, not specifying the topic, and John talked to them at length: it is a carefully organized account of spiritual teaching, beginning with three stories about women, ending with three stories about men, and in between there is a dis-course on the great virtues of the desert, humility, discretion, realism, the 'single eye' of a life directed towards God. The writer first gives three stories he says he had heard from other monks in the district about John: each is about a woman and John's assistance to her. In the first, the wife of a tribune wanted to see John and ask his blessing, which he gave her in a dream. In the second, the wife of another official, an officer in the army, had a baby while her husband was consulting John, and the old man suggested to the father that the child should be called John and sent into the desert to the monks at the age of seven, an instance full of reminiscences of the story of John the Baptist, but perhaps also an indication that the presence of children in the desert was still acceptable.[1] The third story is of the wife of another official who went blind and was cured by the use of oil John had blessed and sent to her. In each case, the woman involved was married and her husband one of the bureaucratic or military population of Roman Egypt. It was the women who asked his help and they received it, though John preserved the usual condition of a monk, in that he did not have direct contact with them. The writer refers to all these as 'strangers', foreigners, and makes a contrast with the other benefits which John gave to the Egypt, ians, his 'fellow-countrymen'. The holy man, in fact, was available to all who needed his help and asked for it, whether from his own district or not.

With this traditional picture of the holy man among his disciples and among both countrymen and strangers, the writer comes to the account of his own visit with the six companions to John. The old man, in spite of a cordial welcome, began with the rebuke already mentioned. One of the company had tried to pretend, out of a mistaken humility, that he was not a deacon, and John corrected him, with the fundamental realism of the desert. 'Do not lie', he said, 'by denying the gift of Christ'. In other words, ordination is only that, a gift; it is not a personal possession making one in any way super, ior, and to deny it is both arrogant, by presuming that it is something owned and prestigious, and also deceitful, contrary to truth in its simplest form. His severity, it seems, did not stop there. Another of the party had a fever, and was told by John that 'this affliction was to his advantage and had come to him because of the weakness of his faith', though he eventually offered help by giving the brother some oil with which to rub himself, a combination of medicine with encouragement which was effective.

John continued to deal austerely with his guests: though he praised, in a wry fashion, their energy in coming to the desert, he added, 'do not imagine that you have done enough . . . do not trust in yourselves . . . be careful . . . that you are not hunting out our virtues for the sake of vainglory'. They were warned against the false values, the desire to seem good rather than be good, the attitude of the visitor to monasteries, by which in giving an account of what has been seen there, the guest somehow attracts to himself praise, treat, ing the monks and his experience of them as something to be grasped and used for his own exaltation.

With this personal and immediate application of the central teaching of the desert, John began a more formal discourse: it followed the same theme of reality, the stripping of illusion, the continuous life-long struggle, in serious, ness and tenacity, to 'see God', to become, 'the friend of God'.[2] The work of the monk is presented as that and that only, and John, while he never claimed that this was the only Christian vocation, was extremely alert to the tempta, tions that other ways of life present to those who have chosen the monastic path. He told the guests three stories to illustrate the dangers and temptations of the monk and these are worth examining in detail for the insight they offer into the ideals of the desert. First, there is the monk who lived in complete solitude in a cave and had followed for years the most extreme traditions of asceticism. 'He had', says the writer, 'given proof of the strongest asceticism', proof, not just claims. He was visited one day by a beautiful woman who tempted him to sin and induced him to accept her advances, only to reject him with mockery which the writer describes as the laughter of the demons. Such a situation was by no means unknown in the desert[3] but in this case the monk is unable to repent; he despairs and returns to the world, a proof to the one telling the story that from the beginning his asceticism was false and not aimed at the fundamental reality of the loss of selfassurance and the gaining of reliance upon the mercy of God. He had used asceticism as a possession for himself, not as a means of grace and so he failed totally.

The second story presents the figure of a man who, on the contrary, had lived in the city and 'done many evil deeds and sinned gravely'. Struck with compunction, and the writer uses the word *penthos,* one of the most weighted of all words in the spiritual vocabulary, he goes to the desert and lives in one of the tombs.[4] His temptation to leave the place and return to the world is graphically described in terms of torment and lacerations at the hands of 'the demons of his former life'; his relations try to persuade him to give up, but he perseveres in this situation of tension and combat, until he is able to live in peace. The biblical text the writer uses to describe his state is, significantly, 'whosoever humbles himself shall be exalted' (Luke 14.11).

In the third story, a monk of outstanding virtue, and of real holiness, becomes conceited and confident in his way of life, as if it were for his own glory; he then becomes slack about its details, including that perennial minor difficulty of the monk, a disinclination to get up promptly in the morning. At last, aware of his decline in fervour, though not yet truly repentant for the real failure of the heart, he leaves the cell and goes into the desert, dissatisfied and restless. There he meets some monks who treat him as 'their true father' and ask his advice and help. The monk speaks to them, giving advice about perseverance until death, and is at once struck by the irony and hypocrisy of his own words. Alone again, in a cell, he returns to prayer but now in real humility and earnestness, as a sinner before his Saviour, not as a wise man of special abilities. The final word of the story completes the pattern of desert monasticism: 'God has accepted your repentance', he is told, 'and has had mercy on you. In future take care that you are not deceived. The brethren to whom you gave spiritual counsel will come to console you, and they will bring you gifts. Welcome them, eat with them, and always give thanks to God'.

Other stories continue these themes throughout the book: the essential beginning in repentance, compunction, the piercing of the heart by sorrow, the need to leave what is binding and constraining, the desert as the image of freedom, the essential realism of conflict with the self and the truth that this too can be only another way of building up the ego unless there is genuine asceticism of the heart, the context of love and friendship as the final solution of the monastic life. The imagery of the demons is often used, as these stories show, to analyse and describe the temptations of monks. This needs perhaps a word of elucidation. The reality of wickedness is usually presented in this literature in terms of demons, and this is so in each of these stories; but this should not lead one to suppose any naivety in the desert fathers; on the contrary, they were the experts of the ancient world in the psychology of the spiritual life. When a demon is mentioned, it is not a simplistic attempt to fill a gap in the narrative by imaginary imps; the fathers were probably well aware of immediate cause and effect, of, for instance, the woman in the first story as a real woman,[5] the torments in the second as the real memories of the past, the mysterious bread of the third as real enough bread from a known source. But they were not concerned with the question 'how', with the mechanics of events; even if known, they were not what the stories were about. What they are describing is a situation of temptation and fall, of evil, sin, despair, and the narrow ways of repentance and return, and in this the image of the demon had a recognised place, saying more that any amount of explanation and with a vivid, resonant effect in the narrative. A real woman might be known to have tempted a monk but the story of this would be about the temptation, not about the woman. It is a complex and subtle matter to discern what is being said in any narrative, especially where the understanding of certain images has been lost.

John of Lycopolis uses these stories and the rest of the discourse to direct his visitors away from unreality towards the true values that come with the attention of the heart to God. He tells them to 'cultivate stillness and train yourselves for contemplation'; the monk who does this, he says, 'stands unimpeded in the presence of God, without any anxiety holding him back; for such a man spends his life with God'. This statement of the aim and method of the ascetic life is reaffirmed in the Latin text of the *Historia Monachorum* by Rufinus where another version of the sermon by John of Lycopolis is given. It deals with the interior life in a very striking way, going directly to that major concern of the desert: thoughts. 'We must take the greatest care over our feelings and our thoughts', John says, 'in the hard and prolonged work of renouncing inner desires, as we stand before God to pray'. The need to renounce not only possessions but the desire for them is presented as the central work of the monk. John describes the rooted selfish-ness that coils round the heart like a serpent, continually burrowing deeper and creating a false and illusory self which is continually restless and un-stable. It is a self which we mistake for our real self; it is precious to us, and we resist the thought of uprooting it; we cover it over, he says, with empty cheerfulness or vain sadness, an idea also stressed in the 'Degrees of Hu-mility' in the *Rule of St Benedict*. The restless heart is contrasted with the inner well of peace and stability which is the work of the Spirit of God, whose presence produces those typical virtues of the desert, love, meekness, long-suffering, not judging others. John has also some sharp words for those who persist in the unreality of conceit and only want to seem good, by quoting what others have had to say rather than undertaking the hard work of ascetism for themselves. The first work of a monk, he says, is prayer to God, so that standing before God who is darkness the false self may be stripped away and the true image and likeness of God within be revealed.

This statement of the ascetical path of the monk, then, forms the first and longest section of the *Historia Monachorum* in both Greek and Latin versions. The rest of the narrative continues the theme, and it is amply supported from other sources as the basic spirituality of the desert fathers. It is not the exercise of asceticism in itself which is fundamental to this way of life, but repent-ance, *metanoia*, the turning from the cultivation of the ego, the eradication of self-will throughout life in abandonment to the cross of Christ. The monk is the sinner, the prodigal returning from a far country, and this return is at first physical and practical, as well as ultimately spiritual. The stories that follow are of men who have actually turned away from the domesticity of life and have gone away, in a more or less dramatic fashion, from the situa-tion in which they have lived. Patermuthius had been a robber and a mur-derer; Philemon the flute-player had taken part in pagan ceremonies and excesses; several robbers became monks under the influence of Theon; there was a brigand who was converted by Apollo and another by Paph-nutius, while some came from a more mundane background. What is stressed is the necessity for leaving a situation of involvement and in one story at least this radical break is described in terms of martyrdom, of a physical struggle almost to death. But this initial separation is only one side of *metanoia* for the monk; to take the body away is only a beginning of conversion. More prolonged attention is given here, as elsewhere, to the fight against the passions, the interior sinfulness of man. The monk, says Apollo, communi-cates as a sinner and receives forgiveness continually from Christ. The monks might be seen by their neighbours as the 'peace-makers', but they saw them-selves as the 'poor in spirit', 'those who mourn', and they had a very different opinion about seeing the face of God.

These men turn, then, from anti-social behaviour; they turn also from the ordinary ways of society, in order to stand before God and search their own hearts to come closer to the reality of themselves. They are men who recog-nise, therefore, that they are broken, incomplete, and they learn to remain incomplete, with their raw edges reaching always towards the heavens. The stories in this text of long fasts, vigils, silence, loneliness, temptation, are not seen as an end in themselves. Apollo severely censured those who wore iron chains and let their hair become unkempt: 'these make an exhibition of themselves,' he said, 'and chase after human approbation'. It is only that which leads to the interior path of repentance that is recommended and here there is agreement between this text and the other literature of the desert. The monk, like Jacob, wrestles in the night with God who is unknown in a life-time's effort and discipline. As the Prologue says, the writer witnessed 'their fer-vent love and great ascetic discipline', in that order. The place of the desert is presented as permanently the place of the cross: the monk 'will stand be-side the Crucified with confidence, for the crucified Lord became obedient unto death'.[6]

> A brother asked an old man, 'How can I be saved?'. The latter took off his habit, girded his loins and raised his hands to heaven, saying, 'So should the monk be: denuded of all things in this world, and crucified. In the contest the athlete fights with his fists; in his thoughts the monk stands, his arms outstretched in the form of a cross to heaven, calling on God. The athlete stands naked when fighting in a contest; the monk stands naked and stripped of all things, anointed with oil and taught by his master how to fight. So God leads us to the victory'.[7]

But if the tears of the monks and the stories of their pain forms the central part of these texts, it is nevertheless not the whole of them. The cell of the monk is called the 'furnace of Babylon' but is also said that there 'the three children found the Son of God'.[8] There is in the *Historia Monachorum*, as in other desert literature, the other side of the cross which is resurrection. The message of the monks is not their own worthlessness but the everlasting faithfulness of God. God, they say, does not lie and he is continually present with the monk, turning his sorrow into the joy of the kingdom. Jacob, to continue the image, wrestles with God in darkness and, permanently crippled, he goes towards the brother he has betrayed and says to him, 'Seeing your face is like seeing the face of God' (Genesis 33. 10). So there is in this text the image of the new Adam restored to heaven in the midst of his trials, not subsequent to them. There are images of light and joy, the life of the angels, sounds of heavenly mirth. The monks are not encountered as gloomy men obsessed with their own asceticism but as those who are more alive and approachable because of it. Even their physical appearance shows the new life that is within them. After forty years of solitude, John of Lycopolis is described as having 'a bright and smiling face'. Bes is described as meek, gentle and utterly serene; Theon went out at night in order to give water to the wild animals; in Nitria, Ammonius welcomed those who came to the community with a feast:

> Those who intended to live in the cells were invited to the church for a feast. And while they were still enjoying themselves, each brother filled his cloak or his basket with loaves or other suitable things from his own cell and brought them to the new ones, so that no one should know which gifts had been brought by which brother.

There was the old man called Didymus who was said to be a man of 'charming countenance', in spite of his unappealing habit of treading on scorpions with his bare feet. Another monk who made an impression on the visitors by his cheerfulness was Apollo, and he told them that happiness was not an option but an obligation for Christians:

> He used to say, 'Those who are going to inherit the kingdom of heaven must not be despondent about their salvation. The pagans are gloomy,' he said, 'and the Jews wail, and sinners mourn, but the just will rejoice . . . we who have been considered worthy of so great a hope, how shall we not rejoice without ceasing?'

The idea is that it is the duty of those who are redeemed by Christ to allow the new life they find in him to be apparent; personal despair is not to be passed on to others but used by the monk in his relationship with the God who gives life and hope.

Another side of this life which comes from heaven is charity and especially charity towards the brothers. The monks were renowned for the loving welcome they gave to guests and there are instances in this text of such hospitality, from the Prologue onwards. The most striking is the description of the reception given to the visitors in Nitria and Cellia, in the Latin version of Rufinus:

> What can I say that would do justice to their humanity, their courtesy, and their love; . . . Nowhere have I seen love flourish so greatly, nowhere such quick compassion, such eager hospitality.

But visitors went away again, and charity to them was limited; what was permanent was the relationship between the monks. The desert, says the Prologue, is a place where 'they are separated in their cells but united in love'. There are instances here of the care of the brothers for each other in need, even of the pleasure they might take in talking with each other, and above all there are instances of that great virtue of the common life, the refusal to pass judgment on others. The most striking story of this is found elsewhere:

> A brother at Scetis committed a fault. A council was called to which Abba Moses was invited but he refused to go to it. Then the priest sent someone to say to him, 'Come for everyone is waiting for you,' So he got up and went. He took a leaking jug filled it with water and carried it with him. The others came out to meet him and said to him, 'What is this, father?' The old man said to them, 'My sins run out behind me and I do not see them, and today I am coming to judge the errors of another'.[9]

The ability attributed to Macarius to 'cover the faults he saw as though he did not see them'[10] is, in all this literature, the fruit and proof of prayer; it has its parallel here in the story of Apollonius the Martyr and his refusal to resent the mockery of Philemon.

Another side of the charity of the desert is also found in this text in the stories of the solitaries who return after many years to take part in the common life with the brothers. For instance there is John who began his life as a wandering hermit pursuing many extremes of asceticism but who then returned in order to direct other monks. Helle also lived a life of extreme solitude but then returned to live with the monks. Or and Apollo both began life as solitaries and both received visions in middle age suggesting that they should return to the monasteries in order to help the brethren. The last story told by John of Lycopolis, of the ascetic who had lived alone and who had been very much tempted in the desert, shows how he eventually returned to cenobitic life for his own good after a vision in which it was said to him, 'God has accepted your repentance and has had mercy on you. In future take care that you are not deceived. The brethren to whom you gave spiritual counsel will come to console you, and they will bring you gifts. Welcome them, eat with them, and always give thanks to God.' The desert is not presented as a place for misanthropes, eccentrics, individualists; it is rather as the Prologue says, 'A place where they are separated in their cells but unified in love'. There is an unfussy charity between the monks, and a dependence of each upon all.

Finally, there is another aspect of this life of sorrow and happiness in pursuit of 'the one thing necessary'; that is, the idea of paradise. The orientation of the monks is towards heaven, towards the life of another world. For this reason they are frequently referred to in this text as angels, as living the angelic life. Or looked 'just like an angel'; Bes had 'attained the angelic state'; and in the Prologue to the text the monks are described as 'while dwelling on earth in this manner they live as true citizens of heaven', they are waiting, 'in expectation of the coming of Christ'. While this eschatologi, cal aspect of the monastic life is stressed here as elsewhere, there is also a less familiar side to it in this text. This is the idea of a visit to the earthly paradise. Patermuthius was said to have been transported physically to paradise and to have brought back a large fig as proof. A more detailed story is told of Macarius, in which he visits the earthly paradise created by the Egyptian Magicians mentioned in the Old Testament, Jannes and Jambres.[11] Several stories are conflated here and Macarius is said to have found a walled paradise in the midst of the desert, in which were two holy men in a garden. He stayed there for several days, eating and talking with them, and finally returned carrying fruit from the paradise; after wandering in the desert he reached his monastery where he tried to persuade his monks to go back there with him. The monks' reply contains all the courtesy and diplomacy of the desert:

> 'if we were to enjoy it in this life, we should have received our portion of good things while still on earth. What reward would we have afterwards when we come into the presence of God? For what kind of virtue shall we be recompensed?' And they persuaded Macarius not to return.

The idea of paradise as a garden full of good and refreshing things to eat perhaps reflects one of the preoccupations of the monks in the dry and re, stricted life of the desert. Certainly there are other stories of visitors who are called 'angels' who supply the monks with food, which is described usually as some kind of rare and exotic fruit while they are in the desert. The control of the appetite was never over; it is instructive that it is gluttony as much as sexuality which was their continuous field of battle.

The 'single eye', and the heart at rest, is presented in this account as the end and purpose of the monk; perhaps the best summary is the description of Bes, who is presented as 'having attained the angelic state', the summit of perfection: 'he lived a life of the utmost stillness, and his manner was serene . . . He was extremely humble and held himself of no account. We pressed him strongly to speak a word of encouragement to us, but he only consented to say a little about meekness, and was reluctant to do even that.'

NOTES TO CHAPTER IV

1. For the presence of children in the desert cf. *Sayings of the Desert Fathers,* Carion 2 and 3; it appears even from this story that boys were already held to be a temptation to the monks, a theme which emerges more strongly later.

2. Cf. *Life of St Antony,* 4.

3. Cf. *Wisdom of the Desert Fathers,* trans. Benedicta Ward, SLG Press, Oxford, 1979, §§ 31–59, pp. 7–21

4. For the use of tombs by Egyptian hermits see the *Life of St Antony,* 8.

5. Cf. *HM* XIII for a story in which the author speaks of 'the devil in the guise of a woman'; Apelles was tempted by her and branded her face with a red-hot iron; the fact that 'the brethren heard her screaming in the cell' is sufficient indication that a real woman was involved.

6. *Sayings of the Desert Fathers,* Hyperechios 8.

7. *Wisdom of the Desert Fathers,* § 11, p. 3.

8. Ibid. § 74, p. 24.

9. *Sayings of the Desert Fathers,* Moses 2.

10. Ibid. Macarius 32.

11. The earthly paradise referred to in Exodus 7.11 ff. and 2 Tim.3.8. This story is told in *Lausiac History* c. XVIII: 'the garden-tomb of Jannes and Jambres ... they built the work with stones four feet square. They erected their monument there and put away much gold. They even planted trees there, for the spot was damp, and they dug a well there too.'

CHAPTER V

A SENSE OF WONDER:
MIRACLES OF THE DESERT

The *Historia Monachorum* contains material which is instructive for social life in fourth-century Egypt, for monasticism in its exterior aspects in Egypt, and for the spiritual and moral approach of visitors to Egypt in recording the account of the lives of the monks. But a more dominant element in this material is the perspective that it gives upon another reality, of a world within and beyond this world, which lay across the Thebaid. One of the elements in the whole literature of early monasticism which is perhaps especially unfamiliar to the modern reader is the account it gives of miracles. There are more miracles in the *Historia Monachorum* than there are in other accounts of a similar kind. As with any literary record of the miraculous it is of course impossible to ascertain the degree of the strictly miraculous or supernatural in such stories; but there is no question that those recording them believed that in some way God had intervened in affairs. How and to what extent it is not always so easy to say. It is, however, possible and very profitable to examine these miracles in their literary form, in order to see what they are intended to say and to form some idea of the approach to such matters in the minds of both the writers and of the participants of these events.

It is first as well to ascertain what kind of vocabulary was used in Greek and in Latin which we translate as 'miracles'.[1] The word *miraculum* and the word *teras* are not those most used. Usual words in the *Historia Monachorum* for miracle are *dunamis, sēmeion, thaumata*; and *signa, virtus, prodigia* and some-times *thaumaturgia*. These events are not seen primarily as *mirabilia*, as things to be wondered at for their strangeness, as being contrary to the course of nature. They are signs, and signs of the power of God. They are, moreover, signs that God is working as strongly now as he did among the prophets and apostles. They illustrate the *virtus* of the monks, and place them directly in the line of the biblical revelation of the power of God.

These events are then signs of something else. First of all, they are signs that point backward to the established authority of relevation in the Scrip-tures. The fathers 'raised the dead and walk on the water like Peter', says the writer. Copres is said to have endured an ordeal by fire against pagans, in a scene instantly reminiscent of Elijah and the prophets of Baal. Apollo and his companions were visited by an angel in prison like Saint Peter. John of Lycopolis is constantly called a prophet. The sun stands still for Patermuthius as it did for Gideon. Bread was provided in the wilder, ness, as for Elijah when he could go no further. This was a way of guarantee, ing the authenticity of events. Such references were a link back with the holy past which was seen in an unbroken line with the present.

The second thing that the monks were clear about was that even though the miracles were in a sense guaranteed by the Scriptures, they were not confined to a remote past. The monks were in the tradition of the prophets and apostles, and as the Prologue says, they 'show that even in these times the Saviour performs through them what he performed through the apostles and prophets'. When Satan appeared to Apollo and said, 'Are you not Elijah or one of the other prophets or apostles?' The old man replied, 'Was God present then but is now away on a journey? God can always do these things, for with him nothing is impossible'. The *dunamis,* the power, now stood over a new Israel in the wilderness. And all that concerned the monks was that miracles should not be a temptation towards pride in themselves but should be seen to be entirely the work of God.

With that overall perspective of the glory of God present now as then, what were the miracles of individuals, and why are they recorded? They can be placed in four categories. There are the miracles of clairvoyance; the miracles of healing; miraculous dreams and visions; and 'nature' miracles. Each of these is a sign, and it is vital to remember this when reading any part of this text: the question 'why', 'what for', is always predominant over the question 'how', 'what are the mechanics of this', in the mind of the ancient world.

To take the miracles of clairvoyance first: as has been said, they were recorded primarily as instances of insight and foreknowledge as great as that of the prophets. John of Lycopolis is said to have been able to predict the future, and so to be in the line of prophets, taking prophecy in its strict and literal sense. He is also said to have been one who could read hearts, one of those who discern reality, one who understands human nature so well that it seems miraculous to the hearers. It is a gift of God, which the writer sees as a result and reward of a life of asceticism. The people who told the visitors about John's prophetic gifts were believed in a similar vein, that is, because they were men of good lives and virtues; they were those who could discern correctly. John and Eulogius therefore were the ones able to read thoughts and to know the dispositions of disciples; Apollo knew that the strangers were visiting him in the desert before they arrived, which seemed miraculous both to them and to his disciples. Theon was said to possess the gift of pro' phecy. John of Lycopolis, like other monks, had the uneasy task of advising an emperor about his military campaigns, and his success in this seemed to be evidence of the miraculous gift of prophecy rather than mere shrewdness and foresight. What is important to see is what the accounts are intending to convey, and that is not a concern with a magical trick of crystal'gazing but a picture of insight and foresight carried by grace to a remarkable degree.

Secondly there are the dreams of the desert. The dream holds a vital place in ancient literature and one which is perhaps only being rediscovered today in certain methods of psychological analysis. There are two things to be noted about the dreams recorded in this account, first the extreme caution exercised by the monks about dreams. The danger of deception was held to be remarkably high in the matter of what was supremely personal and there' fore unverifiable. The demons, as they put it, were more likely to produce dreams and visions than God. Thus, the monks are cautious, the personal revelation is instantly mistrusted and tested: why, after all, should humble monks and sinners, they said, be granted visions? Or, for instance, sees in a dream the demon king and routs him by the name of Christ; the hermit John is offered Communion by Satan and recognises him at once as the adversary. But secondly, dreams were also their natural language for the moments of crisis, the turning points, the moments of vital change, which are dramatised and focused in sleep. There are in the *Historia Monachorum* many instances of this: Or, Apollo, and the hermit John are all noted as dreaming of an angel, or of the voice of God, advising them to go and minister to their brethren after they have been hermits for many years, In two cases it is interesting to note the other strand of the dream, which is the link with the promises of God to Abraham, the father of many. The conversion of Patermuthius to monastic life has the classic form of a dream: asleep in the process of house'breaking, he saw Christ riding by as the Emperor, offering him a place in his army. Philemon the flute'player likewise had his conver' sion confirmed by a dream of the tribunal of Christ, where he saw that the prayers of Apollonius on his behalf were accepted. Apollo saw his natural brother interceding for him to Christ among the apostles and so foretelling his death. For death was the supreme change, the supreme passing over of the limits of life, and for that angels, saints and most significantly martyrs, were seen to come and claim the hermits for their own. In another way, the three dreams of Paphnutius, in which he was shown who were his equals in virtue, came from a deep anxiety about himself and his way of life. These dreams, then, could be good, and the fathers themselves would appear in visions, as when John of Lycopolis appeared in a dream to a woman who wanted to see him face to face, a dream in which Rufinus says that he also cured as well as rebuked her. It is a story which is told from the side of the woman instead of by John and is equally understandable in these terms. The ancients were not, after all, foolish. Sometimes there was doubt about a vision; most significantly of all there was doubt in the minds of the monks who met Macarius on his return from his supposed visit to the paradise of Jannes and Jambres. There seems to be no doubt that they thought it had been a delusion and, in any case, they could not see what advantage it would be to them in their monastic life.

Thirdly, there are the cures. There are very few direct instances of this in the *Historia Monachorum*. There are general comments that some of the holy men were famous for cures: John of Lycopolis blessed oil to anoint the sick; Elias and Or drew crowds for cures; Theon would lean out of the window of his cell to bless the sick; Apollo, John the hermit, Macarius and Amoun are all said to have been visited by crowds of the sick in search of healing. These stories show that the location of power in the individual Christian holy men, who were thought to have special influence with God the creator and sustainer of the world, is a feature of Egypt in the fourth century where the monk was seen as a visible icon of Christ. The heresy of anthropomorphism was after all a popular, domestic idea among the fellahin; and those who saw Origenism as a threat were usually the simple monks to whom God had a human face. Nor were crowds of sick people seeking cures from holy men a monopoly or invention of the Christians. What would be surprising would be if there were no accounts of the sick surrounding the great ascetics. But to look closely at the few instances of cures in the *Historia Monachorum* is to obtain a rather different idea of the monk as thaumaturge than that at first suggested by the text: John of Lycopolis, for instance, is told that one of the visiting monks is ill and needs his help; he says he will not heal him, saying the illness is useful to this monk in teaching him humility and patience, the real virtues of the monastic life. Copres deprecates any claim he had as a healer, saying it is a very small thing to heal the body, something 'even doctors can do'. There is the story of the girl so deluded that she thought she was a horse, in which story Macarius applied the psychological treatment of separation and isolation with prayer and anointing; this story in the version by Rufinus is perhaps even more interesting, since Macarius says that the idea that she is a horse is a delusion and projection by those who in fact are lusting after her. Another cure which is mentioned in the desert is one performed by Amoun: he says that a child suffering from rabies was brought to him having been bitten by a mad dog; Amoun suggests to his patients that the remedy lies in a social act: 'give back to the widow the ox which you have killed surreptitiously, and your child will be restored to you in good health.' Amoun does not make this the cause of the cure of the child; he merely makes it a condition which must be fulfilled before he will pray for the child; the cure is thus given a social context of which the recovery of the child is seen as a part.

The power of God in a saint was called upon by men to remedy that part of the human creation which was in need through sickness. It was a part of the restoration of human nature redeemed in Christ, the new Adam, in which mankind is again perfect and whole in the context of creation. This theme of paradise restored is continued in the fourth class of miracles, those I have called 'nature miracles'. These are miraculous acts which deal with the matter of this world rather than with people. The first and most appealing in this class is the connection of the monk-saints with animals. A world which took the supernatural for granted—and the *Historia Mona-chorum* contains at least one account of the view the monks had of the worship of animals which they assumed was part of the pagan religion of Egypt before their time—was used to seeing a holy man as a focus of power to which all needs, physical, mental, or social, could be brought to be put into contact with the supernatural. The question was, where is divine power to be found? How does one come across it? And then how will it work? So there are stories of the *locus* of the holy being so powerful that it extends to animals, in a restoration of man to the state of paradise, to the situation of the first Adam, restored in Christ the second Adam, once more purified by obedience and therefore at home with the whole of creation. There is the story of Bes talking gently to a hippopotamus and then to a crocodile, and urging them to be at peace and not to ravage the lands of men. Theon was said to go out at night into the desert in order to give water to the gazelles, the antelopes and the wild asses. Amoun asked two serpents to keep guard at his cell; and Helle made a crocodile serve as his ferry over the Nile. Most appealing of all, is the story of Macarius, who cured the blind cubs of a hyena and received in return that sheepskin which later came into the pos-session of Melania.[2] The emphasis, however, in these stories is not on a sentimental attachment to animals but upon the true control and obedience of man and the beasts. Thus, a disciple of Apollo boasted of killing snakes with his hands; Didymus was praised for crushing scorpions with his bare feet; Amoun used serpents as guards but also destroyed those that threatened human lives; and Helle, after using a crocodile as a ferry across the Nile, decided, rather ungratefully one might think, that it was better off dead.

The holy man is at one again with restored creation, but in a right order, in which man is in control and is the crown.

There are other instances of Adam restored to paradise in these stories. There are monks who are fed with the food of paradise and guided by the light of heaven. The holy bread was given, it was said, as miraculous food to those fasting in the wilderness; the parallel with Elijah is often specific. Patermuthius, for instance, was given a mysterious loaf to eat each week; Or was fed by an angel for three years; Apollo received bread at Easter; and Helle was given both bread and dates by an angel. So closely was this image linked with virtue, that when a monk fell into negligence about his life, he saw that the miraculous bread of God degenerated at the same time. It is a vivid concrete image connected with the concept of fasting as feeding on the word of God, broken to men in the Scriptures and in prayer. The theory is that the less a man eats, the closer he becomes to being fed like Adam or like Christ in the wilderness with the bread of God which is the word of God. Similarly, the hermits are said to receive 'light' in the contemplation of God, an image influenced perhaps by the Origenist tradition, which has an important part in the *Historia Monachorum*. In the case of Patermuthius, about whom the 'tallest' stories are told by a deliberate device of Copres, who exaggerates these stories to make his own deeds look less by comparison, the sun stood still so that he reached his destination in daylight, an allusion to Gideon for whom the sun stood still in battle. For Patermuthius it was a sign in his lifelong contest with the demons of darkness. These stories provide examples, above all, of the layers of imagery in these texts; the close connection between images and reality throughout this literature is never to be interpreted simply and only at its face value.

Finally, another kind of miracle to be mentioned is the judgements which are said to fall miraculously upon sinners through the hermits. The figure of the holy man as a focus for spiritual power and arbitration has already been discussed. Concerning the instances of miraculous punishments in the *Historia Monachorum* two things can be said. First, who makes the connection? The observers, the writer, the visitors, but not the holy man himself. An earthquake, for instance, destroyed the house of the garrison commander who imprisoned Apollo, but it was after no threat of his; and it was the man himself who saw it as a judgement connected with his treatment of the Christians. Secondly, the punishments were very often connected with the conversion of pagans through visions, perhaps providing a spiritual kind of shock-treatment needed in order to ensure conversion. Thus, the idol seen by Apollo remains immovable, robbers are unable to move when trying to rob a holy man's house, a thief cannot cook vegetables which he has stolen. The stories

are saying that interior volition, power of action, has been impeded by contact with that which is holy; and in each case conversion, that is, coming
to terms with the new experience of the holy, restores motion and life.

A sense of wonder in the desert is a major feature of these stories of miracles.
The writer hastens to claim for himself a degree of credulity more extreme
than that which he expects of his readers and probably more than that of
those about whom he wrote. What the stories show is the expression of two
great themes, the alliance of the holy men with the powers of heaven so that
they are a cross-section through which heaven looks; and the unimportance
of external acts of power of which there are glimpses; to quote from Cassian,
what is fundamental to their theme is 'not the performance of wonderful
works, but the purity of love'.[3] The work of the monk produces the fruits
of charity and this is the concern of the monks and of those who visited
them. They have little to say about the experiences of prayer which lie over
the threshold of asceticism; perhaps the only hint they give is found in the
story of Joseph of Panephysis:

> The old man stood up and stretched his hands towards heaven. His
> fingers became like ten lamps of fire and he said, 'If you will, you can
> become all flame'.[4]

The experience of God who is darkness is rightly left without words. What
is described in this text is the basic way of life by which a man continually
turns towards God, in one place and at one time, remaining there for one
thing alone. A saying ascribed to Pachomius summarises the concerns of
the monks and their lack of interest in the spectacular:

> If you see a man pure and humble, that is a great vision. For what is greater
> than such a vision, to see the invisible God in a visible man?[5]

It is the 'vision' for which the visitors came to Egypt and it is that 'vision'
alone which they have recorded.

NOTES TO CHAPTER V

1. For an excellent summary of the terms used in the Bible to denote 'miracle' see
   C. Moule, *Miracles,* Appendix 1, London, 1945, where the conclusions are
   the same as those drawn from monastic documents. See the forthcoming
   article by B. Ward: 'Miracles and the Desert Fathers' in the *Proceedings of the
   VIIIth International Patristic Conference* at Oxford, 1979.

2. *Lausiac History* c. XVIII.

3. Cassian, *Conferences* XV 2.

4. *Sayings of the Desert Fathers,* Joseph of Panephysis 7.

5. *Sancti Pachomii Vitae Graecae,* ed. Halkin, *Subsidia Hagiographica* 19, Brussels, 1932, *Vita A,* Cap. 48.

THE LIVES OF THE DESERT FATHERS

PROLOGUE

1. Blessed be God 'who desires all men to be saved and to come to the knowledge of the truth'. (1 Tim. 2.4) For he brought us to Egypt and showed us great and wonderful things which are worthy of being remembered and recorded. He granted to us who desire to be saved both the foundation[1] and the knowledge of salvation. He provided us not only with a model of the good life but also with an exposition[2] sufficient to arouse the soul to devo׳ tion. He gave us a noble testimony to the way of virtue.[3]

2. I myself am not worthy to undertake such an exposition, because it is not appropriate for humble men to treat of great themes.[4] Their powers are not equal to the task of explaining the truth in a fitting manner, particularly when they presume to commit themselves to writing and give inadequate expression to difficult matters. Since we are of no account, it is too presump׳ tuous and dangerous for us to proceed at once to write on this most sublime theme. Nevertheless, the pious community[5] that lives on the holy Mount of Olives[6] has asked me repeatedly to write them an account of the practices of the Egyptian monks which I have witnessed, their fervent love and great ascetic discipline.

I have therefore trusted in their prayers and presumed to apply myself to the composition of this narrative so that I too should derive some profit from the edifying lives of these monks[7] through the imitation of their way of life, their complete withdrawal from the world, and their stillness,[8] which they achieve through the patient practice of virtue and retain to the end of their lives. **3.** For I have truly seen the treasure of God hidden in human vessels.[9] I did not wish to keep this to myself and conceal something which would benefit many. On the contrary, I have contributed my profit to the common fund, for I consider that this transaction, the sharing of what I have gained with the brethren, will be to my advantage, because then they will pray for my salvation.

4. I shall therefore begin this work with the coming of our Saviour Jesus Christ[10] and with the assertion that it is by his teaching that the Egyptian monks regulate their lives. **5.** For in Egypt I saw many fathers living the angelic life as they advanced steadily in the imitation of our divine Saviour. I saw new prophets who have attained a Godlike state of fulfilment by their inspired and wonderful and virtuous way of life. For they are true servants of God. They do not busy themselves with any earthly matter or take account of anything that belongs to this transient world. But while dwelling on earth in this manner they live as true citizens of heaven. **6.** Some of them do not even know that another world exists on earth, or that evil is found in cities. For them the almighty Lord's saying, 'Much peace have those who love thy law,' (Ps. 119.165) is a reality. Many of them are aston⸗ ished when they hear what goes on in the world, for they have attained a complete forgetfulness of earthly affairs.

7. One can see them scattered in the desert waiting for Christ like loyal sons watching for their father, or like an army expecting its emperor, or like a sober household looking forward to the arrival of its master and liberator. For with them there is no solicitude, no anxiety for food and clothing. There is only the expectation of the coming of Christ in the singing of hymns.[11] **8.** Consequently, when one of them lacks something necessary, he does not go to a town or a village, or to a brother, or friend, or relation, or to parents, or children, or family to procure what he needs, for his will alone is sufficient. When he raises his hands to God in supplication and utters words of thanksgiving with his lips, all these things are provided for him in a miraculous way.

9. Why should we speak at length about their faith in Christ, seeing that it can even move mountains? For many of them have stopped the flow of rivers and crossed the Nile dry⸗shod. They have slain wild beasts. They have performed cures, miracles and acts of power like those which the holy prophets and apostles worked. The Saviour performs miracles through them in the same way. Indeed, it is clear to all who dwell there that through them the world is kept in being, and that through them too human life is preserved and honoured by God.

10. I also saw another vast company of monks[12] of all ages living in the desert and in the countryside.[13] Their number is past counting. There are so many of them that an earthly emperor could not assemble so large an army. For there is no town or village in Egypt and the Thebaid which is not sur⸗ rounded by hermitages[14] as if by walls. And the people depend on the prayers of these monks as if on God himself. Some of them live in desert caves, others in more remote places.[15] **11.** All of them everywhere by trying to outdo each other demonstrate their wonderful ascetic discipline. Those in the remotest places make strenuous efforts for fear anyone else should surpass them in ascetic practices.[16] Those living near towns or villages make equal efforts, though evil troubles them on every side, in case they should be considered inferior to their remoter brethren.

12. Accordingly, since I have derived much benefit from these monks, I have undertaken this work to provide a paradigm and a testimony for the perfect, and to edify and benefit those who are only beginners in the ascetic life.[17] 13. Therefore, if God wills, I shall begin this account with a description of the way of life of the holy and great fathers, and show that even in these times the Saviour performs through them what he performed through the prophets and apostles. For the same Lord now and always works all things in all men. (cf. Heb. 13.8; 1 Cor. 12.6)

I ON JOHN OF LYCOPOLIS

1. In the territory of Lyco[1] in the Thebaid[2] we visited the great and blessed John,[3] a truly holy and virtuous man. From what he did it was obvious
to everyone that he possessed the gift of clairvoyance. To the most pious
Emperor Theodosius[4] he not only predicted everything that God was going
to bring about in the world but also indicated the outcome, foretelling the
rebellion of the tyrants[5] against him and their subsequent swift destruction, and also the annihilation of the barbarians who had burst into the
empire.

2. A similar story is told of a general[6] who went to see him to inquire
whether he would overcome the Ethiopians,[7] who at that time had fallen on
Syene[8]—which stands on the frontier of the Thebaid—and had devastated
the surrounding country. John said to him, 'If you march against them, you
will take them by surprise and defeat them and subdue them and you will
find favour with the emperors.' And that is what actually happened, the
event proving as John had predicted. He also said, 'The most Christian
Emperor Theodosius will die a natural death.'[9]

3. The fact that this father[10] really did have an extraordinary gift or
clairvoyance was corroborated for us by the fathers who lived near him,
whose way of life is held in high esteem by all the people of that region.
Whatever they said about the man was not in the least embellished to en-
hance his reputation, but on the contrary tended to be understated.

4. For example, a tribune[11] went to see him and begged him to allow his
wife to visit him too. She desired very much to see him because she was
about to go up-stream to Syene and wanted the father to intercede for her
and send her on her way with a blessing. The father, however, who was
about ninety years old and had not seen a woman throughout the forty years
which he had already spent in the cave, neither going out himself nor allowing a woman to come into his sight, refused to see the tribune's wife. 5. As a
matter of fact not even male visitors ever entered into his cave. He merely
gave his blessing through the window and in this way greeted those who
came and spoke with each of them about his personal affairs.

6. The tribune, however, persisted in pressing him to send for his wife—
for the father lived on the desert escarpment[12] about five miles from the city.
But John would not agree. He said that such a visit was out of the question
and sent the man away crestfallen. Despite this, his wife did not stop pestering

him every day, swearing on oath that under no circumstances would she set out on the journey without seeing the prophet. 7. The woman's oath was reported to the blessed John by her husband. Perceiving her faith, he said to the tribune, 'I shall appear to her tonight in a dream, and then she must not still be determined to see my face in the flesh.' (cf. Col. 2.1) The man told his wife what the father had said. 8. And indeed while she slept the woman saw the prophet coming towards her. He said to her, ' "Woman, what have I to do with you?" (John 2.4) Why have you desired to see my face? Am I a prophet, or do I stand in the ranks of the just? I am a sinful man and of like passions with you. (cf. Acts 14.15) Nevertheless I have prayed for you and for your husband's household, that you may walk in peace according to your faith.' With these words, he disappeared.

9. When the woman woke up, she repeated to her husband what the prophet had said and described his appearance. Then she sent a message of thanks to him by her husband. When he saw him again, the blessed John anticipated his news, saying to him, 'See, I have fulfilled your request. When I saw her I gave her confidence no longer to desire to see me but to go on her journey in peace.'

10. The wife of another high-ranking officer[13] was expecting a baby. While her husband was away, on the very day when he was speaking with Father John, she gave birth, and losing consciousness, hovered on the brink of death. The saint announced this to her husband, saying, "If you knew the gift of God," (John 4.10) namely, that a son has been born to you today, you would glorify God. His mother, however, has come very near to losing her life. When you go home you will find the child seven days old and you will name him John. Bring him up in the knowledge of God,[14] and when he has reached his seventh year send him to the monks in the desert.'

11. These are the wonders which he performed before strangers who came to see him. As regards his own fellow-citizens, who frequently came to him for their needs, he foreknew and revealed things hidden in the future; he told each man what he had done in secret; and he predicted the rise and fall of the Nile[15] and the annual yield of the crops. In the same way he used to foretell when some divine threat was going to come upon them and exposed those who were to blame for it.

12. The blessed John himself did not perform cures publicly. More often he gave oil to the afflicted and healed them in that way. For example, the wife of a senator[16] who had lost her sight through developing cataracts on her corneas asked her husband to take her to the saint. When he told her that the saint had never spoken with a woman, she begged only that he should be told about her and offer a prayer for her. This he did, and more-

over sent her some oil. She bathed her eyes in the oil only three times and on the third day regained her sight and publicly thanked God.

13. But what need is there to speak of any of the works of this saint other than those which we perceived with our own eyes? We were seven brothers, all of us foreign, who went up to see him. When he had embraced us and welcomed each of us with a bright smiling countenance, we asked him at once, before anything else, to say a prayer for us. For this is the custom of the Egyptian fathers. 14. He, however, asked whether anyone in our party was a cleric. When we all replied that none of us was, he looked at us all in turn and knew who was secretly in orders. And indeed one of us had been raised to the diaconate, though only one of the brethren was aware of this, and he had told him not to tell anyone for the sake of humility and because in comparison with such saints he scarcely considered himself to be worthy of the name of Christian, let alone the rank of deacon. Then pointing to him the saint declared, 'This one is a deacon'. 15. But as the brother con-tinued to deny it and tried to remain concealed, the saint reached out through the window, took his hand and kissed it and admonished him, saying, 'Do not spurn the grace of God, my child, and do not lie by denying the gift of Christ. For a lie is something alien regardless of whether its matter is grave or light. And even if one lies with the intention of attaining some good, it is nevertheless not praiseworthy, for the Saviour said that a lie "cometh of evil".' (Matt. 5.37; John 8.44) The brother, having been proved wrong, remained silent and accepted his mild rebuke.

16. We then prayed, and when we had finished praying one of our num-ber, who had already been suffering from a fever for three days, asked to be healed. The father said to him that for the present this affliction was to his advantage and had come to him because of the weakness of his faith. However, he gave him some oil and told him to rub himself with it. When he did this he brought up through his mouth all that was in his stomach, and, delivered of the fever, walked to the guest cell without any assistance.

17. One could see the saint already in his ninetieth year with his body so completely worn out by his *ascesis*[17] that even his beard no longer grew on his face. For he ate nothing apart from fruit, and after sunset at that, in spite of his advanced age, having formerly lived a life of great ascetic discipline. And he never ate bread or anything that needed to be cooked.

18. When he invited us to sit down, we thanked God for our meeting with him. He for his part, after welcoming us like his own dear children after a long absence, addressed us with a smiling face in the following words: 'Where are you from, my children? Which country have you travelled from to visit a poor man?'[18] 19. We told him where we were from, adding, 'We

have come to you from Jerusalem for the good of our souls, so that what we have heard with our ears we might perceive with our eyes[19]—for the ears are naturally less reliable than the eyes—and because very often forgetfulness follows what we hear, whereas the memory of what we have seen is not easily erased but remains imprinted on our minds like a picture.'[20]

20. The blessed John replied, 'And what remarkable thing did you expect to find, my dearest children, that you have undertaken such a long journey with so much labour in your desire to visit some poor simple men who possess nothing worth seeing or admiring? Those who are worthy of admiration and praise are everywhere: the apostles and prophets of God, who are read in the churches.[21] They are the ones you must imitate. 21. I marvel at your zeal,' he said, 'how taking no account of so many dangers you have come to us to be edified, while we from laziness do not even wish to come out of our cave.

22. 'Well now,' he said, 'even though your undertaking deserves praise, do not imagine that you have done enough, that you have achieved something good, but imitate the virtues which our fathers are practising. And if you have attained them all, which is rare, do not on that account trust in your-selves. For some who have been confident in this way, and have approached the very summit of the virtues, have in the end fallen from their position of eminence. 23. On the contrary, be sure that your prayers are going well, that the purity of your understanding has not been sullied, that your mind does not suffer distractions when it appears before God in prayer, lest any unto-ward thought insinuate itself into your mind and turn it towards something else, lest any recollection of indecent images disturb your understanding. 24. Be sure that you have renounced the world according to God's truth, that you have not come "to spy out our liberty", (Gal. 2.4) that you are not hunting out our virtues for the sake of vainglory, so that like men displaying their talents you may appear to others to be imitators of our works. 25. Be sure that no passion[22] disturbs you, or honour and glory and human praise, or the simulation of priestly virtue[23] and self-love, or the thought that you are righteous, or boasting about righteousness, or the memory of any of your relatives when you pray, or the recollection of some happy experience or of any other emotion, or even the remembrance of the world itself as a whole. Otherwise the entire undertaking becomes pointless when, in conversing with the Lord, one is seduced by opposing thoughts.

26. 'Everyone who has not renounced the world fully and completely but chases after its attractions suffers from this spiritual instability. His pre-occupations, being bodily and earthly, distract his mind through the many enterprises in which he is engaged. And then, absorbed in his struggle

against the passions, he cannot see God. However, one should not try to explore this knowledge[24] in any great depth, for fear that one should be granted some small part of it and being unworthy of such a gift should think that one has apprehended the whole, and so fall away utterly to perdition. **27.** On the contrary, it is necessary that one should always approach God in a moderate and devout manner, making spiritual progress according to one's capacity and within the bounds permitted to men. The will, then, of those who seek God must be free from all other concerns. For Scripture says, "Be still and know that I am God." (Ps. 46.10). **28.** Therefore, he who has been granted a partial knowledge of God— for it is not possible for the whole of such knowledge to be received by anyone—also attains to the knowledge of all other things. He sees mysteries, for God shows him them; he foresees what belongs to the future; he contemplates revelations like the saints did; he performs mighty works; he becomes a friend of God, and obtains from God everything he asks.'

29. The saint taught us much else about *ascesis*, including the following: 'One should await death as a transition to a happy life and not look ahead to the feebleness of the body. And one should not fill the belly even with ordinary things—for a man,' he said, 'who is satiated suffers the same temptations as those who live in luxury—but try through *ascesis* to free the appetites from passion.[25] And let no one seek his ease and convenience but let him be strong now and suffer affliction that he may inherit the breadth of the kingdom of Christ. **30.** For Scripture says, "We must through much tribulation enter into the kingdom;" (Acts 14.22) "Because strait is the gate and narrow is the way which leadeth unto life, and few there be that find it;" (Matt. 7.14) and, "Wide is the gate and broad is the way that leadeth to destruction, and many there be which go in thereat." (Matt. 7.13) Why should we be faint-hearted,' he said, 'in this life, seeing that a little later we shall go to eternal rest?' **31.** And again:[26] 'One should not be puffed up about one's own achievements but always be humble and flee to the furthest parts of the desert if one realises that one is becoming proud. For living near villages has often harmed even the perfect. That is why David after a similar experience, sings, "Lo, I flee afar off and have taken up my abode in the desert; I wait for God who delivers me from faintheartedness and tempest." (cf Ps. 55.7, 8) Many of our own brethren have experienced something similar and through arrogance have failed to reach their goal.

32. 'For example, there was a monk,' he said, 'who lived in a cave in the nearer desert and had given proof of the strongest ascetic discipline. He obtained his daily bread by the work of his own hands. But because he persevered with his prayers and made progress in the virtues, he came eventually to trust in himself, placing his reliance on his good way of life. **33.** Then the Tempter asked for him, as he did with Job, and in the evening presented him the image of a beautiful woman lost in the desert. Finding the door open she darted into the cave, and throwing herself at the man's knees begged him to give her shelter since darkness had overtaken her. He took pity on her, which he should not have done, and received her as a guest in his cave. Moreover, he asked her about her journey. She told him how she had lost her way and sowed in him words of flattery and deceit. She kept on talking to him for some time, and somehow gently enticed him to fall in love with her. The conversation became much freer, and there was laughter and hilarity. **34.** With so much talking she led him astray. Then she began to touch his hand and beard and neck. And finally she made the ascetic her prisoner. As for him, his mind seethed with evil thoughts as he calculated that the matter was already within his grasp, and that he had the oppor﹍ tunity and the freedom to fulfil his pleasure. He then consented inwardly and in the end tried to unite himself with her sexually. He was frantic by now, like an excited stallion eager to mount a mare. **35.** But suddenly she gave a loud cry and vanished from his clutches, slipping away like a shadow. And the air resounded with a great peal of laughter. It was the demons who had led him astray with their deception rebuking him and calling out with a loud voice, " 'Whosoever exalteth himself shall be abased.' (Luke 14.11; 18.14) You once exalted yourself to the heavens but now you have been humiliated and brought down to the depths."

36. 'In the morning he got up, dragging behind him the miserable ex﹍ perience of the night. He spent the whole day in lamentation, and then, des﹍ pairing of his own salvation, which is something he should not have done, he went back to the world. For this is what the evil one generally does: when he overcomes someone he makes him lose his judgement, that afterwards he should no longer be able to raise himself up.

'Therefore, my children, it is not in our interest to have our dwellings near inhabited places, or to associate with women. For meetings of this kind give rise to an unexpungeable memory, which we draw from what we have seen and from what we have heard in conversation. And we must not despair of our salvation and bring ourselves to a state of despondency. For even now many of those who have despaired have not been deprived of the love of God, who is always merciful.

37. 'For example,' he said, 'there was another young man in the city who had done many evil deeds and had sinned gravely. At God's bidding this youth was struck by compunction for his many sins. He made straight for the cemetery, where he bitterly lamented his former life, throwing himself down on his face and not daring to make a sound, or to pronounce the name of God, or to entreat him, for he considered himself unworthy even of life itself. While still living he incarcerated himself among the tombs,[27] and renouncing his own life, did nothing but lie underground and groan from the depths of his heart.

38. 'After a week had gone by, some of the demons which earlier had done such great harm to his life appeared to him in the night, calling out and saying, "Where is that abominable fellow? Now that he has really satiated himself with his debaucheries he has, at an inopportune time for us, sud/denly turned chaste and good, and when he is no longer able to do so wishes to be a Christian and a clean liver. But what good does he expect to attain, laden as he is with our vices? 39. Will you not get up and leave this place at once? Will you not go back with us to your old haunts? Whores and tavern keepers are waiting for you. Will you not come and indulge your desires, since every other hope has been extinguished for you? Judgement will inevitably come upon you quickly if you destroy yourself in this way. Why do you hasten towards your punishment, you wretched man? Why do you strive so hard to make your condemnation come quickly?" And there was much else that they said, for instance: "You belong to us; you are bound to us; you have practised every kind of lawlessness; you have become subject to us all and do you dare to escape? Have you no answer? Do you not agree? Will you not come away with us?" 40. But he simply went on groaning, neither listening to them nor answering them a single word, although the demons stayed with him for a considerable time. Since they gained nothing by repeating the same things over and over again, the wicked demons seized hold of him and tortured his whole body savagely. And having lacera/ted him and tormented him cruelly, they went away leaving him half dead.

41. 'When he recovered consciousness, he continued to lie where they had left him, as motionless as before, and began groaning again. In the mean/time his relations had been searching for him. When they found him and learned from him the cause of his terrible physical state, they thought it best to take him home. 42. But although they tried to force him many times, he strongly resisted them. Again the following night the demons put him to the same tortures, but even worse than before. And again in the same way his own people tried to persuade him to move to another place. But he said that it was better to die rather than live a life polluted by such defilements.

43. 'On the third night the demons came very near to killing the man altogether. They fell on him mercilessly with tortures and maltreated him to his last breath. When they saw that he would not surrender, they withdrew, leaving him, however, senseless. As they departed they cried out, saying,

"You have won; you have won; you have won." And nothing frightening ever happened to him again. On the contrary, he dwelt in the tomb as a pure man without any defilement for as long as he lived, practising the virtue of purity. In this way he was not only held in honour by God, but also gave such striking proof of the power to work miracles that he excited admiration in many and stimulated zeal in them for good works. **44.** As a result of this, a great number of those who had utterly despaired of themselves pur/ sued good practices and lived a virtuous life. They realised in their own lives the text of Scripture which says, "Whosoever humbleth himself shall be exalted." (cf. Luke 14.11; 18.14) And so, my children, first of all let us discipline ourselves to attain humility, since this is the essential foundation of all virtues. At the same time, the remoter desert is also profitable to us for the practice of *ascesis*.

45. 'For example, there was another monk who had settled in the further desert and had practised the virtues for many years. Now it happened that in his old age he was tested by the assault of demons. For this ascetic was particularly devoted to stillness. Spending his days as he did in prayer and hymnody and much contemplation, he saw clear visions of a divine nature, sometimes while fully awake, and sometimes while asleep. **46.** He had almost succeeded in laying hold of the traces of the incorporeal life. (cf. 1 Tim. 6.12) For he did not cultivate the soil; he did not worry about what he had to eat; he did not seek to satisfy his bodily needs with plants, not even with grass; and he did not go hunting for birds or any other animals. Instead, from the day when he abandoned the world for the desert he was filled with confidence in God and took no thought how his body should find nourishment. On the contrary, oblivious to everything, he voluntarily kept himself in the presence of God by a perfect desire, and awaited his departure from the world. He was nourished for the most part with the delight of what is hoped for and not seen. (cf. Heb. 11.1) And neither was his body exhausted by the long duration of this regime, nor did his soul lose heart. On the contrary, he maintained this good state of life in a sober manner.

47. 'However, since God held him in honour, at a prescribed time every two or three days he made a loaf appear on the table,[28] a real loaf which could be eaten. And so whenever the monk felt the pangs of hunger and went into the cave, he found food. After prostrating and eating well he used to go back to his hymns, persevering patiently with prayer and contemplation. He grew spiritually every day, adding to his present virtue and future hope and always advancing towards something better. But he came to be almost certain that the better portion was indeed his, as if he already had it in his grasp. And once this had happened, it only needed a little to make him fall

as a result of the temptation which was to come to him afterwards. **48.**
Why do we not say that he narrowly avoided falling? Because when he
came to this presumption he began without realising it to think that he
was superior to most men, and that he had attained something greater than
others, and having arrived at this opinion he began to trust in himself.
49. Before long there was born in him first of all some small indolence,
so small as not to seem to be indolence at all. Then there developed a more
serious negligence. Then it became just perceptible. For he became more
reluctant to rise from sleep and sing hymns. The work of prayer now became
more sluggish. The singing of psalms was not so prolonged. The soul,'
said John, 'wished to rest. The mind turned its gaze earthwards. Thoughts
became subject to distractions. And perhaps, in the secret recesses of his
heart, he began to plan some wickedness.

'The habits, however, which the ascetic had acquired in the past, the
momentum, as it were, of his initial effort, still restrained him in some way
and for the moment kept him safe. **50.** One day, coming in towards the
evening after his customary prayers, he found the bread on the table which
God had provided for him and refreshed himself. But from this point
onwards he did not shake off those reductions of the time he gave to prayer,
nor did he think that these oversights harmed his zeal. On the contrary, he
supposed it a trivial matter to be only just short of failing in his obligations.
51. As a result of this, a powerful sensual desire seized him and diverted
him by evil thoughts[29] towards the world. However, for the moment he
checked himself until the following day, and turned to his customary
ascesis. Then having prayed and sung hymns, he went into the cave and
found the bread lying there, now not so white or well-prepared but looking
rather grey. He was surprised and a little dismayed; nevertheless he partook
and was refreshed.

52. 'The third night came and the evil returned three times more fiercely
than before. His mind fell upon the thoughts with even greater alacrity,
while his memory composed an image like that of a woman actually present
and lying with him. He had the whole scene in front of his eyes as if all along
he was actually performing the act.[30] However, on the third day he came out
again to do his work and to pray and sing hymns, but he could no longer
keep his thoughts pure. On the contrary, he felt unsettled and turned about
restlessly, glancing this way and that. For the memory of his reflections inter-
rupted his good work. **53.** In the evening he went back in, feeling the need
to eat some bread. He found the loaf on the table, but it looked as if it had
been gnawed by mice or dogs: all that remained was a part of the outer
crust. He then groaned and wept, but not as much as he should have done,

not as much as was needed to check the evil. And since he had not eaten as much as he wanted, he was unable to sleep. **54.** The thoughts then returned in throngs, enveloping him on all sides and battling against his understanding, and quickly taking him prisoner, they dragged him back to the world. Then getting up, he set off for the inhabited region,[31] travelling by night through the desert.

'When dawn broke, the settled region was still far away, but he toiled on, suffering from the burning heat of the sun. He began to look around him, scanning the horizon on all sides to see if a monastery would appear where he could go and refresh himself. **55.** As it happened a monastery did appear. Some pious and faithful brethren received him, and treating him like their true father, washed his face and his feet. Then, after saying a prayer, they prepared a table and invited him with love to partake of whatever they had. When he had eaten his fill, the brethren asked him to speak a word of salva-tion to them and tell them by what means they could be saved from the snare of the devil, (cf. 1 Tim. 3.7) and how they should overcome shameful thoughts. **56.** He, like a father admonishing his children, encouraged them to persevere with their labours, because in a little while they would depart and enjoy ample rest. And telling them many other things about the ascetic life, he edified them greatly.

'When he had finished his admonition, he reflected silently for a moment that although he had counselled others, he had remained without counsel himself. **57.** Then his own failure struck his conscience, and he set off into the desert again at a run, bewailing himself and saying, "Unless the Lord had been my help, my soul had almost dwelt in hell;" (Ps. 94.17) and, "I was almost in all evil;" (Prov. 5.14) and, "They had almost consumed me upon earth." (Ps. 119.87) We may apply to his case the text which says, "A brother helped by a brother is like a strong city and like an impregnable wall." (cf. Prov. 18.19). **58.** From that time he spent the rest of his life in sorrow, bereft of the meal which came from God and gaining his bread by his labour. He shut himself in the cave, and spreading sackcloth and ashes under him, did not rise up from the ground or cease lamenting until he heard the voice of an angel saying to him in a dream, "God has accepted your repentance and has had mercy on you. In future take care that you are not deceived. The brethren to whom you gave spiritual counsel will come to console you, and they will bring you gifts.[32] Welcome them, eat with them, and always give thanks to God."

59. 'I have narrated these things to you, my children, that whether you consider yourselves to be among the little ones or the great ones you may make humility your chief aim in the ascetic life—for this is the first commandment of the Saviour, who says, "Blessed are the poor in spirit, for theirs is the kingdom of heaven" (Matt. 5.3)—and that you may not be deceived by the demons, who raise up images before you. **60.** No, if someone should come to you, whether brother, or friend, or sister, or wife, or father, or teacher, or mother, or child, or servant, first stretch out your hands in prayer, and if it is a phantasm it will flee from you. If either demons or men seek to deceive you by flattery and praise, do not believe them and do not become conceited. **61.** As for me, the demons have often tried to deceive me in this way in the hours of darkness, and have not allowed me either to pray or to rest, raising up images before me throughout the night. And in the morning they have mocked me, falling at my feet and saying, "Forgive us, Abba, for having troubled you all night." But I said to them, " 'Depart from me, all ye workers of iniquity;' (Ps. 6.8; Matt. 7.23) for you shall not tempt a servant of God." (cf Matt. 4.7)

62. 'And so you too, my children, should cultivate stillness and cease- lessly train yourselves for contemplation, that when you pray to God you may do so with a pure mind. For an ascetic is good if he is constantly train- ing himself in the world, if he shows brotherly love and practises hospitality and charity, if he gives alms and is generous to visitors, if he helps the sick and does not give offence to anyone. **63.** He is good, he is exceedingly good, for he is a man who puts the commandments into practice and does them. But he is occupied with earthly things. Better and greater than he is the contemplative,[33] who has risen from active works to the spiritual sphere and has left it to others to be anxious about earthly things. Since he has not only denied himself but even become forgetful of himself, he is concerned with the things of heaven. He stands unimpeded in the presence of God, without any anxiety holding him back. For such a man spends his life with God; he is occupied with God, and praises him with ceaseless hymnody.'

64. The blessed John narrated these things to us and much else besides, conversing with us for three days until the ninth hour, and healing our souls. Then he gave us gifts and told us to go in peace, uttering a prophecy that 'Today the victory proclamation of the pious Emperor Theodosius has arrived in Alexandria announcing the destruction of the tyrant Eugenius,'[34] and that 'The emperor will die a natural death.'[35] These things truly hap- pened as he said.

65. We then went to see a number of other fathers, and while we were with them some brothers came to tell us that the blessed John had died in a won- derful manner.[36] He gave orders that for three days no one would be allowed to visit him, and then, bending his knees in prayer, he died and departed for God, to whom be glory for all eternity. Amen.[37]

II ON ABBA OR

1. Then we went to see another wonderful man in the Thebaid called Abba Or.[1] He was the father of the hermitages of a thousand brothers. He looked just like an angel.[2] He was about ninety years old and had a snowy white beard down to his chest. And his face was so radiant that the sight of him alone filled one with awe. 2. Earlier he had spent much time practising the ascetic life as a solitary in the further desert. Afterwards he organised the hermitages in the nearer desert, and planted a marsh with his own hands—there had been shrubs there originally—so that there should be a plentiful supply of wood in the desert. 3. The fathers who lived near him said to us concerning him: 'There was not a single green shoot here before the father came out of the desert.' He planted this grove so that the brothers who gathered round him should not be forced by some want or other to wander hither and thither. On the con-trary, he made provision for all their needs, praying to God and striving for their salvation, that they should not lack any necessity or have any excuse for indolence. 4. When the father first came to live in the desert he ate herbs and certain sweet roots. He drank water whenever he found it, and spent all his time praying and singing hymns. When he had entered fully into old age, an angel appeared to him in the desert in a dream, and said, 'You will be a great nation, (cf. Gen. 46.3) and a numerous people will be entrusted to you. Those who will be saved through you will be ten myriads. For how-ever many people you win in this world, that is the number you will lead in the age to come. Do not hesitate at all,' the angel told him. 'Provided you call upon God, you will never lack anything you need to the end of your life.' 5. On hearing this, he hastened to the nearer desert, where he lived first as a solitary. He built himself a small hut, and contented himself simply with pickled vegetables,[3] frequently eating only once a week. He was originally illiterate, but when he came out of the desert to the inhabited region, a special charism was given to him by God and he was able to recite the Scriptures by heart.[4] Indeed, when a book was given to him by the brothers, he was able to read it because he was familiar with the Scriptures. 6. He also received another charism, the ability to drive out demons so that many sufferers came to him even against their will, proclaiming publicly his ascetic virtues. And he continued to perform other kinds of cures without

ceasing, so that monks flocked to him from all sides, gathering round him in their thousands.

7. When the father saw us, he was filled with joy, and embraced us, and offered a prayer for us. Then, after washing our feet with his own hands, he turned to spiritual teaching. For he was very well versed in the Scriptures, having received this charism from God. He expounded many key passages in the Scriptures for us, and having taught us the orthodox faith, invited us to participate in the Eucharist.[5] 8. For it is a custom among the great ascetics not to give food to the flesh before providing spiritual nourishment for the soul, that is, the Communion of Christ.

When we had communicated and given thanks to God, he invited us to a meal. He sat down with us and while we ate touched on a number of excellent topics. He said to us, 9. 'I know a man in the desert who did not taste any earthly food for three years: every three days an angel used to bring him heavenly food and put it in his mouth. For him this took the place of food and drink. And I know with regard to this same man that the demons appeared to him in a vision and showed him hosts of angels and a chariot of fire and a great escort of guards, as if an emperor was making a visit. And the 'emperor' said ,"You have succeeded in attaining every virtue, my good man; prostrate yourself before me and I shall take you up like Elijah." 10. The monk said to himself, "Every day I bow before my King and Saviour, and if this were he, he would not have asked this of me." No sooner had he expressed what was in his mind with the words, "I have Christ as my King, whom I adore without ceasing; you are not my king," than the demon disappeared.' He told us these things as if speaking about someone else because he wished to conceal his own manner of life. But the fathers who lived with him said that he was the one who had seen this vision.

11. This man, at any rate, was so renowned among many of the other fathers that when a large number of monks came to him, he called together everybody who lived near him and built cells for them in a single day, one delivering mortar, another bricks, another drawing water, and another cutting wood. And when the cells had been completed, he himself saw to the needs of the newcomers.

12. Once when a false brother[6] came to him who had hidden his clothes, he reproved him in public and produced the clothes for all to see. No one, as a result, dared to lie to him any longer: such was the powerful charism which he came to possess through the number and quality of his virtues. In the church one could see the vast number of monks who lived with him, robed in white like choirs of the just and praising God with ceaseless hymnody.

III ON AMMON

1. We visited another man in the Thebaid called Ammon,[1] the father of three thousand monks, who are also called Tabennisiots.[2] These live a very strict life: they wear sheepskin cloaks,[3] eat with their faces veiled[4] and their heads bowed so that no one should see his neighbour, and keep such a profound silence that you would think you were in the desert. Each one practises his own asceticism in secret: it is only for the sake of appearance that they sit at table, so as to seem to eat, and then they try to avoid being observed by each other. Some of them, after helping themselves to bread, or olives, or whatever else was set before them, raised their hand to their mouth only once or twice, and having tasted once from each dish, were satisfied with such food. 2. Others, chewing their bread slowly and abstaining from everything else without trying to dissemble, practised endurance in this manner. Others ate only three spoonfuls of soup[5] and refused any other food. I marvelled at all these things, as was fitting, and have not neglected the edification which may be drawn from this rule of life.[6]

IV ON ABBA BES

1. Then we saw another old man, called Abba Bes,[1] who surpassed everyone in meekness. The brothers who lived round about him assured us that he had never sworn an oath, had never told a lie, had never been angry with anyone, and had never scolded anyone. For he lived a life of the utmost stillness, and his manner was serene, since he had attained the angelic state. 2. He was extremely humble and held himself of no account. We pressed him strongly to speak a word of encouragement to us, but he only consented to say a little about meekness, and was reluctant to do even that.

3. Once when a hippopotamus was ravaging the neighbouring countryside the farmers called on this father to help them. He stood at the place and waited, and when he saw the beast, which was of enormous size, he commanded it in a gentle voice, saying, 'In the name of Jesus Christ I order you not to ravage the countryside any more.' The hippopotamus, as if driven away by an angel, vanished completely from that district. On another occasion he got rid of a crocodile in the same way.

V ON OXYRHYNCHUS

1. We also went to Oxyrhynchus,[1] one of the cities of the Thebaid. It is impossible to do justice to the marvels which we saw there. For the city is so full of monasteries that the very walls resound with the voices of monks. Other monasteries encircle it outside, so that the outer city forms another town alongside the inner. 2. The temples and capitols[2] of the city were bursting with monks; every quarter of the city was inhabited by them. 3. Indeed, since the city is large, it has twelve churches where the people assemble. As for the monks, they have their own oratories[3] in each monastery. The monks were almost in a majority over the secular inhabitants, since they reside everywhere right up to the entrances, and even in the gate towers. 4. In fact there are said to be five thousand monks within the walls and as many again outside, and there is no hour of the day or night when they do not offer acts of worship to God.[4] Moreover, not one of the city's inhabitants is a heretic or pagan. On the contrary, all the citizens as a body are believers and catechumens, so that the bishop is able to bless[5] the people publicly in the street.

5. The chief officials and magistrates[6] of the city, who distributed largesse to the common people, had watchmen posted at the gates and entrances, so that if some needy stranger should appear, he would be taken to them and receive victuals for his sustenance. And what can one say about the piety of the common people, who when they saw us strangers crossing the agora[7] approached us as if we were angels? How can one convey an adequate idea of the throngs of monks and nuns past counting? 6. However, as far as we could ascertain from the holy bishop of that place, we would say that he had under his jurisdiction ten thousand monks and twenty thousand nuns. It is beyond my power to describe their hospitality and their love for us. In fact each of us had our cloaks rent apart by people pulling us to make us go and stay with them.

7. We saw there many great fathers who possessed various charisms, some in their speech, some in their manner of life, and others in the wonders and signs which they performed.

1. We also saw another father in the desert not far from the city,[1] called Theon,[2] a holy man who had lived as an anchorite in a small cell and had practised silence for thirty years. He had performed many miracles and was held to be clairvoyant by the people of those parts. A crowd of sick people went out to see him every day, and laying his hand on them through the window, he would send them away cured. One could see him with the face of an angel giving joy to his visitors by his gaze and abounding with much grace.

2. Not long before, some robbers had come at night from some distance away to attack him. They thought that they would find a considerable sum of gold hoarded by him, and intended to kill him. But he prayed, and they remained at the door, rooted to the spot, until daybreak. When the crowd came to him in the morning and proposed to burn these men alive, he was forced to speak a single sentence to them: 'Let them go unharmed; if you do not, my gift of healing will leave me.' They obeyed, for they did not dare to contradict him. The robbers at once entered the neighbouring monasteries, and with the help of the monks changed their way of life and repented of their crimes.

3. By grace the man had a competent knowledge of three languages, being able to read Greek, Latin and Coptic, as many told us, and as we discovered from the father himself. For knowing that we were strangers, he wrote on a slate, giving thanks to God for our visit.

4. He ate vegetables but only those that did not need to be cooked. They say that he used to go out of his cell at night and keep company with wild animals, giving them to drink from the water which he had. Certainly one could see the tracks of antelope and wild asses and gazelle and other animals near his hermitage. These creatures delighted him always.

VII ON ELIAS

1. We also saw another old man in the desert of Antinoë,[1] the metropolis[2] of the Thebaid, called Elias.[3] By now he would be a hundred years old. People said that the spirit of the prophet Elijah rested on him. He was famous for having spent seventy years in the terrible desert. No description can do justice to that rugged desert in the mountain where had his hermitage, never coming down to the inhabited region.

2. The path which one took to go to him was so narrow that those who pressed on could only just follow its track, with rough crags towering on either side. He had his seat under a rock in a cave, so that even the sight of him was very impressive. As for the rest, his whole body trembled under the weight of his years. Every day he worked many miracles and did not cease healing the sick.

3. The fathers said of him that no one remembered when it was that he went up into the mountain. In his old age he ate three ounces of bread in the evening. In his youth he had made it his rule to eat only once a week.

VIII ON APOLLO

1. We visited another holy man, named Apollo,[1] in the territory of Hermopolis[2] in the Thebaid, where the Saviour went with Mary and Joseph in fulfilment of the prophecy of Isaiah which says, 'Behold, the Lord rideth upon a swift cloud and shall come into Egypt. And the idols of Egypt shall be moved at his presence and shall fall to the ground.' (cf. Is. 19.1) And indeed we saw there the temple where all the idols fell on their faces on the ground at the entry of the Saviour into the city.[3]

2. Now we saw this man, who had hermitages under him in the desert at the foot of the mountain,[4] and was the father of five hundred monks. He was renowned in the Thebaid and great works were ascribed to him, and the Lord performed many wonders through him, and a multitude of signs were accomplished at his hands. Since from childhood he had given proof of great *ascesis*, at the end of his life he received the following grace: when he was eighty years old he established on his own a great monastery[5] of five hundred perfect men, almost all of them with the power to work miracles.

3. When he was fifteen years old, he withdrew from the world and spent forty years in the desert, scrupulously practising every virtue. Then he seemed to hear the voice of God saying to him, 'Apollo, Apollo, through you I will destroy the wisdom of the wise men of Egypt, and I will bring to nothing the understanding of the prudent pagans. (cf. Is. 29.14) And together with these you will also destroy the wise men of Babylon for me, and you will banish all worship of demons. And now make your way to the inhabited region, for you will bear me "a peculiar people, zealous of good works".' (Tit. 2.14).

4. He replied, 'Take from me, Lord, the sin of arrogance, in case I become overbearing towards the brotherhood and deprive myself of every good.' The divine voice said to him again, 'Put your hand on your neck and you will catch hold of arrogance, and thrust it into the sand.' He quickly put his hand on his neck and grasped a small blackamoor, and thrust it into the sand, as it cried out, 'I am the demon of pride.' And again a voice came to him, saying, 'Go, for whatever you ask you will receive from God.' As soon as he heard this he set off for the inhabited region.

It was about the time of the tyrant Julian,[6] and for a while he lived in the neighbouring desert. 5. He occupied a small cave and dwelt there at the foot of the mountain. His work consisted in offering prayers to God throughout the day, and in bending his knees a hundred times in the night and as many times again in the day. His food at that time, as at the beginning, was provided miraculously by God. **6.** For food was brought to him in the desert by an angel. His clothing was a tunic,[7] which some call a *colobium,* and a small linen cloth wrapped round his head. He had these things with him in the desert for a long time without wearing them out.

7. He dwelt, then, in the desert adjoining the settled region, living in the power of the Spirit and performing signs and wonderful miracles of healing. These were so amazing that they defy description, according to what we heard from the old men who were with him, who were themselves perfect and leaders of large communities.

8. The saint quickly became famous as a new prophet and apostle who had been raised up for our generation. As his reputation grew, large numbers of monks who lived round about in scattered hermitages kept coming to join him, making gifts of their own souls to him as if to a true father. Some of these he invited to contemplation; others he commanded to apply themselves to practical virtue, showing first by deed what he exhorted them to do by word. **9.** Indeed very often, to show them what asceticism meant, he only ate with them on Sundays, otherwise eating nothing more than whatever plants sprang up naturally from the soil. During this time he did not eat bread, or beans, or lentils, or any fruit, or anything that needed to be cooked.

10. Once in the time of Julian he heard that a brother had been taken forcibly for military service[8] and was being kept chained up in prison. He went to see him with the brethren to console him and encourage him to endure his sufferings and take no notice of the dangers which threatened him. 'For now,' he said, 'is the hour of struggle, when the will is tested by the onset of temptations.' **11.** While he was making the brother's soul resolute with these words, the garrison commander appeared, beside himself with evil rage—for someone had informed him about Apollo—and barring the doors of the prison, he put Apollo and all his monks under arrest, thinking that they would make recruits for the coming campaign. Then, having set a strong guard over them, he went off to his own house without allowing their petitions even to reach his ears.

12. At about midnight an angel bearing a torch appeared to the guards, and shed a dazzling light on all who were in the room. At the sight, the guards' mouths fell open with astonishment. They got up and asked all the monks to leave, for the doors had been opened for them, declaring that it was better for them to die for letting them go rather than to disregard the deliverance which had come from God to men imprisoned without cause.

13. Early in the morning the garrison commander came to the prison with his officers and told the men to hurry and get out of the city. For his house, he said, had been destroyed by an earthquake and his servants were buried in the ruins. When the brothers heard this, they went off into the desert singing hymns of thanksgiving to God, and from this time forth all of of them, in accordance with the apostolic saying, had one heart and one soul. (cf. Acts 4.32)

14. He used to teach them every day to excel in the virtues and to drive away at their first appearance those devices of the devil which manifest themselves in evil thoughts. For once the head of a snake is crushed, the whole of its body is lifeless. 'God had commanded us,' he said, 'to be careful of the serpent's head; (cf. Gen. 3.15) this is so that we should not allow ourselves to entertain even the first suggestion of wicked and indecent thoughts, let alone indulge in sordid mental fantasies. Try, rather, to outdo each other in the virtues, lest anyone should appear to have a lower reputation with regard to their practice than his neighbour. 15. Let it be a sign to you of progress in the virtues,' he said, 'when you have acquired mastery over the passions and the appetites. For these are the beginning of the charisms of God. When someone receives proof from God that he can work miracles, let him not be puffed up with pride, reckoning that he has reached perfection, and let him not be elated with the thought that he has already been honoured more than the others, and let him not show everyone that he has obtained such a charism; otherwise, stripped of his good sense, and deprived of grace, he simply deceives himself.'

16. These are the profound truths which he taught in his discourses and which subsequently we also heard ourselves from his own lips. But in his deeds he accomplished greater things, for when he prayed, everything he asked for was immediately granted to him by God. He also saw visions. For example, he saw his own older brother who had himself become perfect in the desert and had given proof of a life of even greater ascetisism than his own. Apollo himself had spent many years with him in the desert. 17. Now in a dream he saw him seated on a throne beside the apostles— he had left him his virtues as an inheritance—and he was interceding with God for him, entreating him to take him quickly from this life and give him rest with him in heaven. But the Saviour said to him, 'He needs to spend a little longer on earth to attain perfection, until he has gained many zealous imitators of his way of life. For a great nation of monks is to be entrusted to him, a pious army, that he may receive from God the credit which his labours deserve.' 18. That is what he saw and what indeed came to pass. Many monks flocked to him from every quarter because of his renown; and

inspired by his teaching and manner of life, a vast number of people renounced the world.

A community of brothers formed itself around him on the mountain, as many as five hundred of them, all sharing a common life and eating at the same table. **19.** One could see them looking like a real army of angels, drawn up in perfect order, robed in white, and realising in their own lives the text of Scripture which says, 'Be glad ye thirsty desert; break forth into singing thou that didst not travail with child; for more are the children of the desert than the children of the married wife.' (Is. 31.1; 54.1) Of course this prophetic saying has been fulfilled with regard to the entry of the gentiles into the Church. **20.** But it has also been fulfilled with regard to the many children which the Egyptian desert presents to God, more than those of the settled regions of the earth. Where in the cities are there so many companies of the saved as these armies of monks which the deserts of Egypt present to God? There are as many monks in the deserts as there are laymen in the rest of the world.

It seems to me that one of the Apostle's sayings has also been fulfilled with regard to these monks, the one which says, 'Where sin abounded, grace did much more abound.' (Rom. 5.20). **21.** For at one time a gross and obscene idolatry abounded in Egypt, more than in any other nation. For the Egyptians worshipped dogs and apes and other animals, and considered garlic and onions and other common vegetables to be gods, as I heard from the holy Father Apollo himself when he spoke about them and explained the reason for the polytheism which was once prevalent[9]. **22.** 'Our pagan predecessors,' he said, 'deified the ox, for example, because by means of this animal they carried on their farming and produced their food. They deified the water of the Nile because it irrigated the whole countryside. They also venerated the soil because theirs was more fertile than any other land. **23.** 'As for the remaining abominations, dogs and apes and the whole loathsome collection of animals and vegetables, they worshipped these because their preoccupation with them was the cause of their salvation in the time of Pharaoh, keeping the people busy when Pharaoh was drowned in his pursuit of Israel. Whatever preoccupied each person and prevented him from following Pharaoh, that is what he deified, saying, "This has today become my god, for it was through this that I did not perish together with Pharaoh." ' That is what Saint Apollo taught in his discourses.

24. But rather than dwell on his discourses, I ought to write about the powers which he manifested in his works. For there were once pagans living near him in all that region, and the neighbouring villages in particular practised the idolatrous worship of demons. **25.** There was a huge temple in one of the villages which housed a very famous idol, though in reality this image was nothing but a wooden statue. The priests together with the people, working themselves up into a bacchic frenzy, used to carry it in procession through the villages, no doubt performing the ceremony to ensure the flooding of the Nile.[10] 26. It so happened that on one such occasion Apollo passed by that place with a few of the brothers. As soon as he saw the crowd passing in a frenzy through the countryside as if possessed by devils, he bent his knees and prayed to the Saviour, and at once stopped all the pagans in their tracks. Although they pushed one another, no one was able to advance any further from that spot. All day they roasted in the hot sun, at a loss to explain what had happened to them. Then their priests said that there was a Christian in their territory who dwelt in the desert; he was the cause of this—they were referring to Apollo—and they must entreat him; otherwise their lives were in danger.

27. When the villagers who lived nearby heard the voices and the general uproar, they came up to them and asked, 'What is this that has come upon you so suddenly? How did such a thing occur?' They said that they did not know, but they suspected that Apollo had caused it, and added that they must appease him. The villagers confirmed that they had indeed seen him go by. 28. But since they pleaded with them to help them without delay, the villagers brought up oxen and attempted to move the idol. However, the idol remained totally immovable, as did the priests themselves. Then, unable to think of any other solution, they sent an embassy to Apollo by means of their neighbours with the message that if he would free them from that place they would renounce their error.

29. When this was conveyed to him, the man of God came down to them as quickly as he could, and having prayed, loosed the bonds of them all. As a body they all rushed towards him, committing themselves fully to belief in the Saviour of the universe and the God who works miracles, and at once set fire to the idol. When he had catechised them all, he handed them over to the Christian congregations. Many of them entered monasteries and are still living there today. Apollo's fame spread rapidly in all directions and many believed in the Lord. As a result, there is no longer anybody in his district who may be termed a pagan.[11]

30. Not long afterwards, two villages came into armed conflict with each other in a dispute concerning the ownership of land. When Apollo was informed of this, he went down to them at once to restore peace among them. 31. The opposing party would not be persuaded but kept contradicting him because they had put their trust in a brigand chief whom they reckoned a first-class fighter. Seeing that this man was opposing him, Apollo said to

him, 'If you obey me, my friend, I shall ask my Master to forgive you your sins.' When the brigand heard this, he did not hesitate. He threw down his arms and clasped the saint's knees. Then Apollo, having become a mediator of peace, restored to each person his own property.

32. When peace had been restored among them and they had gone home, their famous champion followed the saint, entreating him to give him some proof that the promise had been fulfilled. Taking him into the neighbouring desert, the blessed Apollo gave him spiritual instruction and encouraged him to have patience, saying that it was possible for God to grant him what he wanted. 33. When night fell, they both had a dream in which they were suddenly present together at the tribunal of Christ, and they both saw the angels and the just prostrate before God. When these two had also fallen on their faces and worshipped the Saviour, a divine voice addressed them, saying, ' "What communion hath light with darkness, or what part hath he that believeth with an infidel?" (2 Cor. 6.14, 15) Why has the murderer come into my presence with the just man when he is unworthy to contemplate such a sight? Now depart from me, my friend, for this suppliant of untimely birth has been pardoned for your sake.' 34. Then they saw and heard a host of other wonders, such as the tongue does not dare to utter or the ears to hear, and when they woke up they related their experience to their companions. Everyone thought it an extraordinary thing that both of them described the same vision. The man, now a murderer no longer, remained with the monks to the end of his days, having amended his life as if he had been changed from a wolf into an innocent lamb. 35. In him was fulfilled the prophecy of Isaiah which says, 'Wolves and lambs shall feed together, and the lion shall eat straw with the ox.' (cf. Is. 65.25) One could also see negroes at that place practising *ascesis* with the monks. Many of them excelled in the virtues. In them was fulfilled the text which says, 'Ethiopia shall stretch out her hand unto God.' (cf. Ps. 68.31)

36. Another time some pagan villagers were in dispute with some Christians over their boundaries, and a large number on either side had taken up arms. Apollo came to pacify them. He was opposed by the champion of the pagans, a ferocious and bloodthirsty man who swore that he would not make peace as long as he lived. The saint said to him, 'Then let it be as you have chosen. No one else will be killed except you. And when you die the earth will not provide a grave for you, but the bellies of wild beasts and vultures will be gorged on your flesh.' 37. And indeed the word quickly became fact, no one from either side being killed but the champion. They heaped sand over him but found him in the morning dismembered by vultures and hyenas. When they saw this prodigy, how the saint's word

had come true, they all believed in the Saviour and proclaimed Apollo a prophet.

38. Some time before this, Saint Apollo was living in a cave in the mountain with five brothers. He had recently come from the desert and these were his first disciples. Easter came, and when they had finished giving worship to God they ate whatever they happened to have. There were a few dry loaves and some pickled vegetables. **39.** Then Apollo said to them, 'If we have faith, my children, and are true sons of Christ, let each of us ask of God what he desires to eat.' **40.** But they entrusted the whole matter to him, considering themselves unworthy of such a grace. He therefore prayed with a radiant face and they all said 'Amen'. And at once in the night a number of men arrived at the cave, complete strangers to them, who said that they had travelled a long distance. They were carrying things which the brothers had never even heard of before, things which do not grow in Egypt: fruits of paradise of every kind, and grapes and pomegranates and figs and walnuts, all procured out of season, and honeycombs, and a pitcher of fresh milk, and giant dates, and white loaves still warm although brought to them from a foreign country. **41.** The men who brought these things delivered them simply with the message that they had been sent by a rich magnate, and immediately departed in a hurry. The brothers partook of these provisions until Pentecost and satisfied their hunger with them, so that they wondered and said, 'Truly these were sent by God.'

42. One of the monks asked the father abruptly to pray for him that he might be granted some grace or other. When the father had prayed for him, the grace of humility and gentleness was granted to him, so that all were amazed at him and the extraordinary degree of gentleness which he had attained. **43.** The fathers who were close to Apollo narrated these miracles of his to us, and many of the brethren confirmed what they said.

44. For example, not long ago, when there was a famine in the Thebaid, the people who lived in the neighbouring district, on hearing that Apollo's community of monks was often fed in a miraculous way, came to him as a body with their wives and children to ask him to bless them and give them food. The father, never fearing that there would be any shortage, gave to each of those who came sufficient food for one day. **45.** When only three baskets of bread were left and the famine still continued, he ordered the baskets which the brethren intended to eat that day to be brought out, and in the hearing of all the monks and the people said, 'Is the hand of the Lord not strong enough to multiply these loaves? For the Holy Spirit says, "The bread from these baskets shall not be consumed until we have all been satisfied with new wheat." ' **46.** And all those who were present confirmed that the bread was sufficient for everybody for four months. And he did the same with oil and with wheat, so that Satan appeared to him and said, 'Are you not Elijah, or one of the other prophets or apostles, that you have the con/ fidence to do these things? 47. But the father said to him, 'Why do you say that? Were not the holy prophets and apostles, who have handed on to us the power to do such things, men themselves? Or was God present then, but is now away on a journey? God can always do these things, for with him nothing is impossible. (cf. Luke 1.37) If God, then, is good, why are you evil? But why should we not declare what we ourselves have also seen: those who brought in the bread placed full baskets on the tables of the brethren, and after five hundred brothers had eaten their fill took them away still full?

48. It is also right to add that we witnessed another miracle which aston/ ished us. Three of our party were on our way to visit the saint. We were seen and recognised from afar by the brethren, who had already heard about our arrival from him. They came running to meet us, singing psalms. For this is what they generally do with all their visitors. And when they had pros/ trated before us with their faces to the ground, they kissed us, and pointing us out to each other, said, 'See, the brothers have arrived about whom the father spoke to us three days ago, saying that in three days three brothers from Jerusalem will visit us.' 49. Some of them went in front of us and others followed behind, singing psalms, until we came near to where the saint was. When Father Apollo heard the sound of singing, he greeted us according to the custom which all the brethren follow. When he saw us, he first pros/ trated, lying full length on the ground; then getting up he kissed us, and having brought us in, prayed for us; then, after washing our feet with his own hands, he invited us to partake of some refreshment. He does this with all the brethren who come to visit him. 50. Those who live with him do not take any food themselves until they have assisted at the Eucharist and re/ ceived Communion.[12] They do this daily at the ninth hour. Then, after having eaten, they sit and listen to the father's teaching on all the command/ ments until the first watch of the night. At this point some of them go out into the desert and recite the Scriptures by heart throughout the night. The rest remain where they are and worship God with ceaseless hymnody until daybreak. I saw them myself with my own eyes begin their hymns in the evening and not stop singing until the morning. 51. Many of them only come down from the mountain at the ninth hour, and having taken part in the Eucharist leave right away, satisfied with spiritual food alone until the ninth hour of the following day. A large number of them do this for many days at a time. 52. Nevertheless, one could see them in the desert filled with a joy and

a bodily contentment such as one cannot see on earth. For nobody among them was gloomy or downcast. If anyone did appear a little downcast,[13] Father Apollo at once asked him the reason, and told each one what was in the secret recesses of his heart. 53. He used to say, 'Those who are going to inherit the kingdom of heaven must not be despondent about their salvation. The pagans are gloomy,' he said, 'and the Jews wail, and sinners mourn, but the just will rejoice. Moreover, those who are occupied with earthly things rejoice in their earthly concerns, but we who have been considered worthy of so great a hope, how shall we not rejoice without ceasing, since the Apostle urges us to rejoice always, and to pray without ceasing, and to give thanks in everything?' (cf. I Thess. 5.16–18) 54. But how can one describe the grace of his speech and all his other virtues, which so amazed us that we fell silent whenever we heard him teach or listened to the others speaking about him?

55. When we were alone with him he taught us much about *ascesis* and how to regulate our lives. And he frequently spoke about the reception of visitors, saying, 'You must prostrate yourselves before brothers who come to visit you, for it is not them but God you venerate. Have you seen your brother? says Sripture; you have seen the Lord your God.[14] 56. 'This,' he said, 'has come down to us from Abraham. (cf. Gen. 18.2) And that we must press the brothers to refresh themselves we have learned from Lot, who pressed the angels in this way.' (cf. Gen. 19.1–3) He also said: 'Monks, if possible, should communicate daily in the Mysteries of Christ. For he who separates himself from the Mysteries, separates himself from God. He who receives Communion frequently, receives the Saviour frequently. For the saving voice says, "He that eateth my flesh and drinketh my blood dwelleth in me and I in him." (John 6.56) 57. 'It is therefore useful for monks to keep the remembrance of the Saviour's passion in their minds constantly, and to be ready every day, and to prepare themselves in such a way as to be worthy to receive the heavenly Mysteries at any time, because it is thus that we are also granted the forgiveness of sins. 58. 'The canonical fasts,' he said, 'must not be broken except under extreme necessity.[15] For the Saviour was betrayed on a Wednesday and crucified on a Friday. He who does not keep these fast days participates in the betrayal and crucifixion of the Saviour. But if a brother comes to you in need of refreshment and it is a fast day, you shall prepare a table for him alone. However, if he does not wish to eat, do not force him. For we all follow the same teaching.

59. He severely censured those who wore iron chains and let their hair grow long.[16] 'For these,' he said, 'make an exhibition of themselves and chase after human approbation,[17] when instead they should make the body

waste away with fasting and do good in secret. Rather than do this, they make themselves conspicuous to all.'

60. However, who could give a full account of his teaching, which reflects his way of life so closely? No one could do it justice either in writing or in speech. 61. During the whole week we were with him he often conversed with us in private, and when we took our leave said, 'Be at peace with one another and do not part company with each other on the road.' Then he asked the brethren who were with him which of them would be willing to escort us as far as the next community of fathers, and almost all clamoured to accompany us. 62. Saint Apollo chose three men, perfect in word and in conduct and familiar with the Greek, Latin and Coptic languages, and ordered them to escort us and not leave us until we were thoroughly satisfied that we had visited all the fathers. But if anyone should wish to see them all, the whole of his life would not be long enough to make a complete tour. Then he let us go with the following blessing: 'The Lord shall bless you out of Zion, and may you see the good of Jerusalem all the days of your life.' (cf. Ps. 128.5)

1. As we were travelling through the desert in the middle of the day, we suddenly noticed the track of a large serpent:[1] it looked as if a log had been dragged through the sand. As soon as we saw it we were gripped with an intense fear. The brothers who were guiding us begged us not to be afraid, but rather to have courage and follow the serpent's track. 'You shall see our faith,' they said, 'for we intend to kill it. We have destroyed many serpents and asps and horned vipers with our bare hands, and have fulfilled in our own lives the Scripture which says, "I gave unto you power to tread on ser/ pents and scorpions, and over all the power of the enemy." ' (Luke 10.19)

2. We, however, unwilling to believe them and by now quite terrified, begged them not to follow the serpent's track but to continue on our way. But one of the brothers, too impatient to wait any longer, left us and rushed off into the desert to hunt down the monster. Upon finding the nest not far away, he shouted to us that the serpent was in the cave, and called us over to him to see what would happen, urging us and the other brothers not to be afraid.

3. As we were going in great trepidation to see the monster, we were suddenly intercepted by a brother, who took us by the hand and led us towards his hermitage. He said that we would not be able to withstand the animal's attack, especially as we had never before seen anything like it, add/ ing that he himself had often seen this monster and it was of enormous size, more than fifteen cubits long.[2] 4. He ordered us to stay where we were, and went to the other brother to persuade him to leave the nest. The brother was all for not moving from the place until he had killed the serpent. However, he prevailed on him and brought him back to us full of complaints about our lack of faith.

5. We stayed to rest with that brother, whose hermitage was about a mile away, and regained our strength. He told us that in that place were he himself had his seat there had lived a holy man called Amoun,[3] whose disciple he had been. Amoun had performed many miracles in that place. 6. He was often visited by robbers, who stole his bread and provisions. One day he went out into the desert and summoned two large serpents. He ordered them to remain in front of the hermitage and guard the door. When the murderers came up in their usual way and saw the prodigy, their jaws dropped open with astonishment and they fell on their faces. 7. When Amoun came out,

he found them unable to speak and almost unconscious. Then raising them up he chided them, saying, 'Do you see how much more ferocious you are than the wild beasts? These, thanks to God, obey our wishes. But you have neither feared God nor respected the piety of Christians.' And bringing them into the cell, he prepared a table for them and exhorted them to change their way of life. They repented at once and went away much better men than they had been before. And not long afterwards they too were seen performing similar miracles.

8. 'Another time,' he said, 'when a large serpent was ravaging the neigh-bouring countryside and killing many animals, the people who live on the edge of the desert all came in a body to the father to entreat him to rid the country of the monster. But since he was unable to help them, he sent them away crestfallen. 9. At dawn, however, he got up and went to the monster's regular run. When he had bent his knees in prayer three times, the snake appeared and hurled itself at him with tremendous force, panting horribly and blowing and hissing and emitting a foul breath. But he, not frightened at all, turned towards the serpent and said, "Christ the Son of the living God, who is destined to destroy the great sea-monster,[4] will destroy you too." 10. As soon as he said this, the serpent burst and vomited through its mouth all its poison mixed with blood. The peasants came when it was day and looked at that great prodigy. But being unable to bear the smell, they heaped a large quantity of sand over the animal. The father remained there with them because they did not dare to approach the serpent even though it was dead.

11. 'One day,' he said, 'when the serpent was still alive, a shepherd boy suddenly saw it, and going rigid with terror, fainted away. The boy lay there unconscious in a field beside the desert the whole day. Towards evening his relations found him, scarcely breathing and swollen from the coma. Not knowing why this had happened to him, they took him to the father. When he had prayed and anointed him with oil, the boy regained consciousness and told them what he had seen. It was this above all that made the saint determined to destroy the serpent.'

X ON COPRES

1. There was a priest[1] called Copres[2] who had a hermitage in the desert not far away. He was a holy man, nearly ninety years old and the superior[3] of fifty brothers. He, too, used to perform a great number of miracles, healing diseases, effecting cures, driving out demons, and working wonders, some of them, indeed, before our very eyes. 2. When he saw us he embraced us and prayed for us, and after washing our feet questioned us about what had been happening in the world. But we asked him rather to explain to us the virtues of his own rule of life, and how God had granted him spiritual gifts, and by what method he had obtained this grace. The priest, without the slightest thought of pride, gave us an account of his own life and that of his great predecessors, who had become much better men than he, and whose manner of life he himself imitated. 'There is nothing wonderful about my own achievements, my children,' he said, 'when they are compared with the rule of life which our fathers followed.'

ON PATERMUTHIUS

3. 'For example, there was a father who lived before us called Patermuthius.[4] He was the first of the monks in this place and was also the first to devise the monastic habit. In his former life as a pagan he had been a brigand chief and a tomb robber, and had become notorious for his crimes. But he found the following occasion of salvation. 4. One night he attacked the hermitage of an anchoress,[5] intending to rob it. By some stratagem he contrived to get himself onto the roof. But not finding any means by which to enter the inner chamber,[6] or alternatively, by which to retreat, he remained on the roof till morning, deep in thought. He slept briefly and in a dream saw someone like an emperor who said to him, "Do not keep watch, pondering on tombs and these petty crimes. If you wish, instead, to change your way of life to one of virtue, and to enter military service with the angels, you will receive the power to do so from me." He accepted joyfully, and the emperor showed him a regiment of monks and entrusted him with their command.

5. 'When he woke up, he saw the anchoress standing near him. "Where are you from, my good man?" she said. "What is your station in life?" He

replied that he knew nothing, and asked her to direct him to the church. She did so, and then throwing himself at the feet of the priests, he asked to become a Christian and to be given an opportunity for repentance. **6.** The priests, since they recognised him, were amazed, but afterwards they admonished him and taught him to be a murderer no longer. He asked them if he could listen to the psalms, but when he had heard only the first three verses of the first psalm, he said that for the time being that was enough for him to learn. After staying with them for three days, he went out and at once hurried off into the desert. He lived in the desert for three years, spending his time praying and weeping, and the wild plants were sufficient for his food. **7.** Then he returned to the church and announced that the lesson had been made effective. For the grace, he said, had been given to him by God to recite the Scriptures by heart. And the priests were once again astonished at him for having attained the highest degree of *ascesis.* They then baptized[7] him and entreated him to stay with them. **8.** But after spending seven days with them, he departed for the desert again. And what is more, when he had completed another seven years in the outer desert, the man was granted a wonderful grace. For every Sunday he found a loaf of bread beside his head. Then he prayed and ate it and was satisfied until the following Sunday.

9. 'He returned from the desert again, giving proof of his *ascesis* and stimulating some to want to go and take up his manner of life. A certain young man went to him, wishing to become his disciple. He dressed him at once in a sleeveless tunic, and having put a hood on his head, a sheepskin cloak on his shoulders, and a linen cloth round his waist, he introduced him to the ascetic life. Now if a Christian happened to die while persevering in asceticism with him, he used to bury him in a seemly manner and keep a vigil. **10.** His disciple, seeing him attending to the burial of the dead in such an admirable way, said to him, "And when I die, will you also bury me in this way, teacher?" And he replied, "I shall bury you in the same manner until you cry out, 'Enough.'" **11.** Not long afterwards the young man died, and the word became fact. For after conducting the funeral with devotion, he asked him in front of everybody, "Have I carried out your funeral rites well, my child, or is there still some detail lacking?" The young man let out a cry in the hearing of many: "I am satisfied, father; you have fulfilled your promise." Astonishment seized those who were present, and they glorified God for what he had done. But the father withdrew to the desert, shunning praise.

12. 'Once he came down from the desert to visit some brothers, former disciples of his, who were stricken with disease, for God had revealed to him that one of them would die. But evening was already approaching and the village was still some distance away. Not wishing to enter the village at night, since he avoided unsuitable times and practised the Saviour's precepts, "Walk while ye have the light," (John 12.35) and, "If any man walk in the day, he stumbleth not," (John 11.9) he addressed the setting sun with the words, "In the name of the Lord Jesus Christ stand still a little in your course, until I arrive at the village." 13. The sun, which had already become a semicircle on the horizon, stood still and did not set until he came to the village. As a result the miracle became obvious to the villagers. They all gathered to watch the sun and marvelled to see that for many hours it did not set. When they saw Father Patermuthius coming out of the desert, they asked him what this miraculous sign could mean. 14. He said to them, "Do you not recall the words of the Saviour: 'If ye have faith as a grain of mustard seed, greater works than these shall ye do?' " (cf. Matt. 17.20; John 14.12) At once fear overcame them, and some of them re‑ mained with him, becoming his disciples.

15. 'He went into the house where one of the sick brothers was, and finding him already dead, went up to the bed and prayed and kissed him and asked which he preferred, to go to God, or to continue to live in the flesh. 16. The brother sat up and said to him, "It is better to depart and to be with Christ. (Phil. 1.23) To live in the flesh is not essential for me." "Then sleep in peace, my child," he said, "and intercede with God for me." The brother, just as he was, immediately lay back and died. All who were present were amazed and said, "Truly this is a man of God." Then he buried him in a fitting manner, and spent the whole night singing hymns.

17. 'He visited another sick brother, and when he saw that he was sorely distressed at his approaching death because his conscience reproached him, he said to him, "In what an unprepared state you go to God, bearing the thoughts of your negligent life as accusers." The brother begged and beseeched him to intercede with God for him, that he might be given a little longer in this world, since he intended to amend his life. 18. The father said to him, "Do you seek an opportunity for repentance now, when your life is over? What have you been doing all your life? Were you not only unable to heal the wounds you have, but even wish to add others?" However, since the brother continued to implore him, he replied, "If you do not add other evils to your life, if you are truly repentant, we shall pray to Christ for you. For he is good and long‑suffering, and he grants you a little longer to live so that you may repay everything." And when he had prayed, he said to him, "Behold, God has granted you three years in this life. Only repent with all your soul." 19. And taking him by the hand, he raised him up there and then and led him into the desert. When the three

years were up, he brought him back to the village and presented him to
Christ no longer a man but an angel, so that all were amazed at his supernatural power. When the brothers had assembled, he set him in the midst
of them in good health and spent the whole night teaching them. Then the
brother began to feel drowsy, and falling asleep, died. After praying for him,
he performed the funeral rites in the proper way and bore him to his tomb.

20. 'It is said that he often stepped out onto the Nile and crossed over to
the other side with the water only up to his knees. Another time he flew
through the air and suddenly appeared where the brethren were on a roof-
terrace, even though the doors were shut. Frequently if there was somewhere
he wished to be, he suddenly found himself there. He once told the brethren
that when he was returning from the desert he was taken up in a vision into
the heavens and saw all the good things that await those who are true monks,
things which no words can describe. 21. He had also been transported
physically to paradise, he said, and had seen a vast company of saints.
He related how he had eaten of the fruits of paradise, and showed evidence
of the fact. For he had brought his disciples a large choice fig, deliciously
scented, to prove to them that what he said was true.' The priest Copres
who was telling us this story, being at that time a young man, saw this fig
in the hands of Patermuthius's disciples, and kissed it, and admired its scent.
22. 'For many years,' he said, 'it remained with his disciples, being kept
as evidence of the father's visit to paradise. It was of enormous size. Indeed a
sick man had only to smell it and he was at once cured of his illness.

23. 'At the beginning of his period of withdrawal into the desert,' he said,
'when he had not eaten for five weeks, he met a man in the desert who was
carrying bread and water. The man persuaded him to eat and disappeared.
On another occasion the devil showed him the treasure-vaults of Pharaoh
full of pure gold. The man said to him, "Thy money perish with thee."
(Acts 8.20)

24. 'These and even greater things,' said Copres, 'were achieved by our
Father Patermuthius while performing signs and wonders. And other such
men have lived before us "of whom the world was not worthy". (Heb.
11.38) What wonder if we lesser men perform the little things that we do,
healing the lame and the blind, which the physicians also accomplish by
their skill?'

25. While Father Copres was telling us these stories, one of our party,
overcome with incredulity at what was being said, dozed off. And he saw a
wonderful book lying in the father's hands, which was inscribed in letters of
gold. And beside the father stood a white-haired man, who said to him in
a threatening manner, 'Are you dozing instead of listening attentively to the

reading?' He immediately woke up and told the rest of us who were listening to Copres, in Latin, what he had seen.

26. While the father was still speaking to us about these things, a peasant carrying a shovelful of sand came up and stood by him, waiting for him to finish his discourse. We asked the father what the peasant wanted the sand for. **27.** He replied, 'My children, I should not have boasted to you or told you about the exploits of our fathers, for fear that we should become puffed up inwardly and lose our reward. However, for the sake of your zeal and edification, because you have come so far to see us, I will not deprive you of what may be edifying, but will explain in the presence of the brethren what God in his providence has effected through us.

28. 'The land bordering us was infertile, and the peasants who owned it scarcely had a double return from the seed which they sowed. For a worm developed in the ear and destroyed the whole crop. Those farmers who had been catechized by us[8] and had become Christians asked us to pray for the harvest. I said to them, "If you have faith in God, even this desert sand will bear fruit for you." **29.** Without a moment's hesitation they filled the folds of their tunics with the sand which had been trodden by us, and bringing it to me, asked me to bless it. After I had prayed that it should be done to them according to their faith, they sowed the sand together with the corn in their fields, and at once their land became extremely fertile, more than anywhere else in Egypt. As a result, it is now their custom to do this, and every year they trouble us for sand.

30. 'There was another great miracle which God performed through me in the presence of many people. Once on going down to the city I came across a certain Manichaean[9] who was leading the common people astray. As I was unable to make him change his mind by debating with him publicly, I turned to the crowd and said, "Light a great pyre in the street and we shall both enter into the flames. Whichever of us is unharmed by the fire will be the one with the true faith." **31.** When this was done and the pyre had been lit, the crowd dragged both of us together to the flames. But the Manichaean said, "Let each of us go singly into the fire. And you must go first yourself," he added, "because you proposed it." I made the sign of the cross in the name of Christ and went into the fire. The flames parted on either side and did not harm me for the half hour which I spent in their midst. **32.** On seeing the miracle, the crowd began to shout and compel the other man to enter the fire in turn. But he was unwilling because he was afraid, and so the mob took hold of him and thrust him into the middle of the fire. He was badly burned all over his body. Then the mob drove him in disgrace from the city, crying, "Burn the charlatan alive!" As for me, the crowd took me with them, and shouting acclamations escorted me to the church.

33. 'On another occasion I was passing by a temple where some pagans were sacrificing to their idols. I said to them, "If, having minds yourselves, you still offer sacrifice to what is mindless, you will then be less endowed with minds than these idols." Judging that I had spoken well, they im/mediately believed in the Saviour and followed me.

34. 'I once had a garden in the countryside nearby, for the sake of the brethren who used to come to us. It was cultivated by a certain poor man. Now one of the pagans broke into it to steal vegetables. When he had taken some he went home. For three hours he tried unsuccessfully to cook them, but they remained in the pot just as he had picked them, without the water even getting warm. **35.** Then coming back to his senses, the man gathered up the vegetables and brought them to us, begging us to forgive him his trans/gression and asking to become a Christian. And that is precisely what happened. Just at that time there were some brothers visiting us, and the vegetables which had been brought to us were exactly what was needed for them. After partaking of them we thanked God for having given us a double joy: both the salvation of the man and the refreshment of the brothers.'

1. 'Once Abba Sourous,'[1] said Copres, 'and Isaiah[2] and Paul,[3] all of them devout men and ascetics, met one another unexpectedly at the river bank as they were on their way to visit the great confessor, Abba Anouph.[4] He lived at a distance of three days walk from them. And they said to one another, "Let each of us demonstrate his degree of spiritual progress and the way in which God honours him in this life."

2. 'Abba Sourous said to them, "I ask as a gift from God that we should arrive at our destination without fatigue in the power of the Spirit." Scarcely had he prayed when a boat was found ready to sail together with a favourable wind, and in the twinkling of an eye they found themselves at their destination, although they were travelling up-stream.

3. 'Isaiah said to them, "We should not wonder, my friends, if the father, when he meets us, tells us what ascetic practices each of us has performed."

4. 'And Paul said to them, "Has not God revealed to us that after three days he will take the saint up to heaven?" When they were only a short distance from the place, the father came to meet them and embraced them. Then Paul said to him, "Tell us what you have accomplished, for the day after tomorrow you will depart for God."

5. 'Abba Anouph said to them, "Blessed be God, who has made known to me too both your visit and your rule of life." After describing the achieve-ments of each of them, he also gave an account of his own virtues, saying, "From the time when I first confessed the name of Jesus on earth no lie has ever come forth from my mouth. I have eaten nothing earthly, for an angel has fed me each day with heavenly food. No desire has arisen in my heart for anything except God. 6. There is nothing hidden on earth which God has not made known to me. Light has never ceased to shine on my eyes. I have not slept in the day, nor have I ceased to seek God at night; but an angel has always been with me, showing me the powers of the world. The light of my understanding has never been extinguished. Everything I have asked from God I have received at once. 7. I have often seen tens of thousands of angels standing before God. I have seen choirs of the just. I have seen companies of martyrs. I have seen armies of monks. I have seen the work of all those who praise God. I have seen Satan delivered to the fire. I have seen his angels handed over to punishment. I have seen the just filled with joy for ever."

8. 'Having spoken to us about these things and much else for three days, he delivered up his soul. At once angels received it, and choirs of martyrs led it up to heaven, while the fathers looked on and heard the hymns.'

1. 'Another father, called Abba Helle,[1] had persevered since childhood in the ascetic life. He often carried fire to his neighbouring brethren in the fold of his tunic, and stimulated them to advance to the point of performing miracles, saying to them, "If you practise true *ascesis*, then show the super-natural signs of virtue."

2. 'On another occasion, when he was alone in the desert, there came upon him a desire for honey. At once he found some honey-combs under a rock. "Depart from me, unbridled desire," he said, "for it is written, 'Walk in the Spirit, and ye shall not fulfil the lust of the flesh.' " (Gal. 5.16) And leaving the honey-combs, he went away. When he had already been fasting for three weeks in the desert, he found some fruit which had been thrown away. But he said, "I shall not eat. I shall not touch a single one of these that I may not scandalize my brother, that is, my soul, for it is written, 'Man shall not live by bread alone.' " (Matt. 4.4; Luke 4.4)

3. 'He fasted for another week and afterwards fell asleep. And an angel came to him in a dream and said to him, "Rise up and take whatever you find and eat it." He rose up and looked about him and saw a spring with tender green plants growing all around it. He drank from the water and ate some of the vegetables and declared that he had never tasted anything more delicious.

4. 'He found a small cave at that place and stayed there for a few days without eating. Then, when he needed food again, he bent his knees and prayed. At once all kinds of victuals appeared on the ground beside him, including warm loaves, and honey, and various kinds of fruit.

5. 'Once he went to visit his own brethren. When he had admonished them well, he hastened back into the desert, carrying some supplies suitable for his needs. On seeing some wild she-asses grazing, he said to them, "In the name of Christ, let one of you come over to me and relieve me of my burden." At once one of them trotted towards him. He loaded her with his baggage, and mounting her himself, arrived at the cave in a single day. When he had laid out the bread and the fruit in the sun, the wild animals which used to come to the spring went up to them. But they had only to touch the loaves and they expired.

6. 'Once on a Sunday he went to see some monks and said to them, "Why have you not celebrated the *Synaxis*[2] today?" When they replied that

it was because the priest had not come from the other side of the river, he said to them, "I shall go and call him." But they said that it was impossible for anyone to cross the ford, partly because of the depth, but most of all because there was a huge beast at that spot, a crocodile which had devoured many people.

7. The father did not hesitate. At once he jumped up and rushed into the ford. And immediately the beast took him onto its back and set him down on the other side. On finding the priest at his place, he entreated him not to neglect the community of brothers. The priest, seeing that he was dressed in a rag with many patches, asked him where he had found it, saying, "You have a most beautiful mantle for your soul, brother," 8. for he was amazed at his humility and poverty. He followed Helle back to the river. As they failed to find a ferry, Helle let out a cry calling the crocodile to him. The animal obeyed him instantly and offered its back as a raft. Helle asked the priest to climb on with him. 9. But the priest was terrified at the sight of the beast and backed away. While he and the brothers who lived on the other bank watched, seized with dread, he crossed the ford with the beast, came ashore, and hauling the beast out of the water, said to it, "It is better for you to die and make restitution for all the lives you have taken." Whereupon the animal at once sank onto its belly and died.

10. 'He stayed on with the brethren for three days. Taking his seat among them, he taught them the commandments and revealed the secret counsels of each of them, saying that one was troubled by fornication, another by vanity, another by self-indulgence, and another by anger. He declared that this man was meek and that that one was a peacemaker, bringing under his scrutiny the vices of some and the virtues of others. 11. On hearing these things they were amazed and said, "Yes, it is just as you say." Then he said to them, "Prepare some vegetables for us. For a large party of brothers will come to us today." While they were still preparing the table, the brothers arrived and embraced each other.

12. 'One of the brethren, desiring to be saved, asked him if he might live with him in the desert. He replied that he would not be able to bear the temptations of the demons, but the brother contradicted him vehemently and promised to bear all things. And so the father accepted him and recommended that he should live in a neighbouring cave. 13. The demons appeared at night and tried to strangle the brother, after first shaking him with obscene thoughts. He ran out of his cave and told Abba Helle all that had happened. The father drew a line round the place and commanded his disciple henceforth to remain in it without fear.

14. 'Once when they had almost exhausted their stock of loaves, an

angel appeared in the cave in the form of a brother and brought them some-thing to eat. Another time ten brothers who were searching for him wandered in the desert for seven days without any food. On finding them himself, he invited them to rest in his cave. **15.** When they mentioned that they had not eaten, the father, having nothing to set before them, said to them, "God is able to furnish a table in the wilderness." (cf. Ps. 78.19) At that moment a servant appeared at the door, a handsome young man, and persisted in knocking while the brethren were at prayer. When they opened the door, they saw that the youth was carrying a large basket full of bread and olives. They received them from him and partook of them, after giving thanks to the Lord, the servant having at once disappeared.'

16. When Father Copres had finished telling us these amazing stories and other things even more wonderful, and had treated us with all customary kindness, he took us into his own garden and showed us date-palms and other fruit trees which he had planted himself in the desert. This had been suggested to him by the faith of those peasants to whom he had said that even the desert can bear fruit for those who have faith in God: 'For when I saw that they sowed sand and their land bore fruit,' he said, 'I tried to do the same and I succeeded.'

XIII ON APELLES

1. We visited another priest in the district of Achoris[1] called Apelles,[2] a just man who in his former life had been a blacksmith and had abandoned his trade to turn to *ascesis*. One day when he happened to be forging utensils for the monks, the devil came to him in the guise of a woman. In his zeal he snatched up a red-hot piece of iron from the fire with his bare hands, and badly seared her face and whole body. **2.** The brethren heard her screaming in the cell. From that time the father was always able to hold red-hot iron in his bare hands without being burned. He received us courteously, and told us about the men worthy of God who had been with him and were still living there.

ON JOHN

3. 'For example, in this desert,' he said, 'there is a brother of ours called John,[3] a man of another age, who surpasses in virtue all the monks of our own time. It is not easy for anyone to find him because he is always moving from place to place in the desert. **4.** He began by standing under a rock for three years in uninterrupted prayer, not sitting at all or lying down to sleep, but simply snatching some sleep while standing. His only food was the Communion which the priest brought him on Sundays. His rule of life permitted nothing else.

5. 'Now one day Satan assumed the form of the priest and went to him earlier than usual, pretending that he wanted to give him Communion. The blessed John, realising who it was, said to him, "O father of all subtlety and all mischief, enemy of all righteousness, will you not cease to deceive the souls of Christians, but you dare to attack the Mysteries themselves?" (cf. Acts 13.10) **6.** The devil replied, "I have only just failed to overthrow you. For it was in this way that I led one of your brethren astray, and when he had lost his wits I drove him mad. Many just men prayed very hard for him and only just succeeded in bringing him back to his right mind." Having said this, the demon left him.

7. 'When his feet had swollen and split from his standing motionless for so long, and the discharge had cause putrefaction, an angel appeared and touched his mouth, saying, "Christ is meat indeed for you and the Holy Spirit is drink indeed. (cf. John 6.55) For the time being this spiritual food is sufficient; otherwise your stomach will become too heavy and you will vomit." 8. And having healed him, the angel made him leave that place. From that day he spent his time in the desert wandering about and eating plants. But on Sundays he was always at the same place to receive Communion.

9. 'He begged a few palm leaves from the priest and wove harnesses for the beasts of burden. There was a cripple who wanted to visit the father, seeking a cure. He mounted the ass, and as soon as his feet touched the strap which had been made by the holy man, he was instantly cured. He sent other gifts to the sick and they were delivered immediately from their infirmity.

10. 'It was once revealed to him with regard to the hermitages under his direction that some of them did not maintain a strict observance. He wrote letters to them all through the priest,[4] saying that these were lax and those zealous for virtue. And it was found that what he said was true. He also wrote to their superiors, saying that some of them were negligent about the salvation of the brethren, while others encouraged them satisfactorily, and he declared the rewards and the punishments of each.

11. Another time he summoned others to a more perfect state of life, suggesting that they should withdraw from sensible things and advance to the things of the spirit: "Now the time has come for us to show evidence of such a way of life. For we must not remain children," he said, "or infants, for ever. On the contrary, we must now devote ourselves to more perfect thoughts, and lay hold of manly resolution, and take the greatest virtues by storm." '

12. The father told us these and other even more marvellous stories about this saint. They are so very extraordinary that we have not written them all down—not because they are not true, but because some people will be sceptical. As for us, we were fully convinced because many great fathers told us these things and had seen them themselves with their own eyes.

1. We also visited the place where Paphnutius[1] had lived as an anchorite. He was a great and virtuous man who had died not long before in the vicinity of the city of Heracleopolis in the Thebaid. Many people told numerous tales about him.

2. This father, for example, after many years of *ascesis* asked God to make known to him which of the saints who had lived a virtuous life he most resembled. An angel appeared and said to him, 'You are like the flute player[2] who lives in such and such a city.' The father eagerly hastened to see him. He set himself to question him about his way of life and to examine all his ascetic practices. **3.** The flute player said to him, which was the truth, that he was a sinner, a drunkard and a fornicator, who not long ago had abandoned the life of a brigand for that of a flute player. **4.** When the father asked him specifically what good deeds he had ever accomplished, he replied that he was not aware of any good action in himself except that once in his days as a brigand he rescued a nun who was about to be raped by a gang of robbers and at night led her back to her village.

5. Then on another occasion he found a beautiful woman wandering in the desert who was being pursued by agents of the governor and the city councillors[3] because of her husband's arrears of taxes[4] and was bitterly lamenting her vagabond life. He asked her why she was crying. **6.** She replied, 'Do not ask me, master; do not question me in my misery but take me anywhere you wish as your handmaid. For my husband has often been flogged during the last two years because of arrears of taxes amounting to three hundred gold coins.[5] He has been put in prison and my beloved three children have been sold as slaves. As for me, I have become a fugitive and move from place to place. I now wander in the desert but I am frequently found and flogged. I have been in the desert now for three days without eating anything.' **7.** 'I felt sorry for her,' said the brigand, 'and took her to my cave. I gave her the three hundred gold coins and brought her to the city, where I secured her release together with that of her husband and children.'

8. Paphnutius said to him, 'I am not aware myself of having accomplished anything equal to this. But as regards *ascesis*, you have no doubt heard that I am famous. For I have not spent my life in ease and self-indulgence. Now God has revealed to me concerning you that as regards virtuous achievements you do not lag behind me at all. And so, brother, if God thinks so

highly of you, do not be negligent and leave your soul's fate to chance.'
9. The man, who was holding his flutes in his hand, immediately threw
them away, and transforming musical harmony into a spiritual melody,
followed the father into the desert. After practising *ascesis* for three years with
all his strength and occupying all the time remaining to him with hymns
and prayers, he departed on the journey for heaven, and numbered with the
choirs of saints and the companies of the just, took his rest.

10. When he had sent this man, who had practised the virtues so well,
on ahead to God, and had set himself a rule of life even more austere than
before, he asked God once more to reveal to him which of the saints he most
resembled. And again he heard a divine voice saying, 'You are like the
head man of the neighbouring village.' 11. He went to him as quickly as
he could. When he had knocked on his door, the man came out in his
customary way to receive him as a guest. Having washed his feet and prepared a table for him, he invited him to have something to eat. But the
father asked him about his virtuous practices, saying, 'Tell me, my friend,
about your way of life. For God has revealed to me that you have reached a
higher state of life than that of many monks.' 12. The man said that he was
a sinner and unworthy to be compared with monks. However, as the father
kept pressing him, he said, 'For my part, I do not feel any compulsion to
describe my own deeds. But since you say you have come from God I
will tell you what my attributes are.

13. 'It is now thirty years since I separated from my wife. I slept with her
for only three years and had three sons by her. These now assist me with my
affairs. I have not ceased to practise hospitality to this day. No one in the
village can claim to be more prompt in offering shelter to a stranger. No poor
man or stranger has gone away from my courtyard empty-handed without
first having been supplied with suitable victuals. I have never come across
anyone destitute without giving him ample relief. 14. I have not taken the
side of my own children when judging a case. Other people's produce has
not entered my house. There has been no dispute which I have not pacified.
No one has blamed my servants for any misconduct. My flocks have not
touched other people's corn. I did not sow my own fields first, but turned
them over to common use and only harvested what remained. I have not
allowed a poor man to be oppressed by a rich man. I have never at any time
in my life hurt anyone's feelings. I have never given a dishonest judgement
against anyone. This is what by God's will I am conscious of having done.'

15. When Paphnutius had heard the man's virtues, he kissed his head,
saying, ' "The Lord shall bless thee out of Zion; and thou shalt see the good
of Jerusalem." (Ps. 128.5) These are wonderful accomplishments. But you

lack one thing which is the crown of the virtues: the all-wise knowledge of God. You will not be able to attain this virtue without effort unless you deny yourself the world, and take up the cross, and follow the Saviour.' (cf. Matt. 16.24; Mark 8.34) As soon as the man heard this, he did not even stop to put his affairs in order but immediately followed the father to the mountain.

16. Now when they came to the river and no boat appeared, Paphnutius ordered him to wade across. No one had ever waded across at that place before because of the depth. After they had crossed over with the water only coming up to their waists, he established him at a certain place, and separating himself from him, prayed to God to reveal which of the two was the greater. 17. Not long afterwards he saw the man's soul borne up by angels singing hymns to God and saying, 'Blessed is the man whom thou choosest and adoptest; he shall dwell in thy courts.' (cf. Ps. 65.4) And the just were saying in reply, 'Great peace have they that love thy name.' (cf. Ps. 119.165) And he knew that the man had died.

18. Paphnutius, however, continued to entreat God with prayers and to prolong his fasts. And again he asked that it should be revealed to him whom he resembled. Again the divine voice said to him, 'You are like a merchant seeking fine pearls. (cf. Matt. 13.45) Now arise and do not delay. For the man whom you resemble is coming to meet you.' 19. So he went down and saw a merchant of Alexandria,[6] a pious Christ-loving man, who dealt in business worth twenty thousand gold coins. He was making his way down-stream from the Upper Thebaid with a hundred ships and distributing all his estate and his merchandise to the poor and the monks. 20. He sent up to the father by his own servants ten sacks of beans and lentils. 'And what are these?' said Paphnutius. The merchant said to him, 'These are the fruits of the commerce in which I have been engaged. I offer them to God for the refreshment of the just.' 'Why, then,' said Paphnutius to him, 'do you not become a monk yourself?' 21. When he confessed that he was eagerly on his way to do just that, Paphnutius replied, 'How much longer are you going to busy yourself with earthly affairs without putting your hand to the things of heaven? Come now, leave these things to others. For your part, make use of this opportunity; follow the Saviour and shortly afterwards you will depart and be with him.' 22. Without the slightest delay he ordered his servants to distribute the remainder of his property to the poor. Then he went up into the mountain and having shut himself up in the cave where his two predecessors had died, he persevered with prayer to God. After a little time had elapsed, he left his body and became a citizen of heaven.

23. When he had also sent this man on ahead to heaven, Paphnutius himself lost the will to live, for he was no longer able to practise *ascesis*. Then an angel appeared to him and said, 'Come now, you blessed one; enter yourself into the eternal tabernacles of God. For the prophets have come to welcome you into their choirs. I did not reveal this to you earlier, for fear that you would become proud and forfeit your reward.' 24. He survived only another day. Some priests came to see him after receiving a revelation. He told them everything and then delivered up his soul. The priests saw him plainly as he was taken up to heaven with the choirs of the just and the angels singing hymns to God.

XV ON PITYRION

1. In the Thebaid we saw a high mountain[1] overhanging the river, a most awesome place with high crags, and we visited the monks who lived there in the caves. Their father, whose name was Pityrion,[2] had been one of Antony's disciples and was the second to succeed him as superior. He performed many different kinds of miracles and was especially noted for driving out demons.

2. When he succeeded Antony and his disciple Ammonas,[3] it was fitting that he should also have received the inheritance of their spiritual gifts. He delivered many discourses to us on a variety of topics, but he spoke with particular authority on the discernment of spirits. He said that there were certain demons which followed the passions and often made us disposed to do evil. 'Therefore, my children,' he said to us, 'whoever wishes to drive out the demons must first master the passions. 3. For whichever passion one overcomes, one also drives out its corresponding demon. You must conquer the passions step by step in order to drive out the demons which belong to them. There is a demon which follows gluttony; if you gain control over gluttony, you will drive out its demon.'

4. The saint ate twice a week, taking on Sundays and Thursdays a little soup made with corn meal. He was not able to eat anything else because his constitution had been conditioned in that way.

1. We also visited another priest called Eulogius.[1] Whenever he offered the sacrifice to God, he received so great a gift of knowledge that he knew the spiritual state of each monk who approached the altar. Often when he saw certain monks about to come up to the altar, he kept them back, saying, 'How do you dare to approach the sacred Mysteries when you entertain wicked thoughts? You, brother; last night you let your mind dwell on obscene thoughts of fornication.[2] 2. Another,' he said, 'has reflected inwardly that it makes no difference whether he approaches the grace of God as a sinner or as a righteous man. And another has had doubts about the sacrifice, saying, "I wonder if it will sanctify me if I approach it?"[3] Abstain for a while from the sacred Mysteries and repent with all your soul that you may win forgiveness for your sins and become worthy of the Communion of Christ. If you do not first purify your thoughts you may not approach the grace of God.'[4]

XVII ON ISIDORE

1. In the Thebaid we also visited a monastery belonging to one Isidore,[1] which was fortified with a high brick wall and housed a thousand monks. Within the walls were wells and gardens and all that was necessary to supply the needs of the monks, for none of them ever went out. The gate keeper was an elder, and he never allowed anyone to go out or to come in unless he wished to stay there for the rest of his life without ever leaving the enclosure. **2.** This gate keeper had a small guest house near the gate where he put up visitors for the night. In the morning he would give them gifts and send them on their way in peace.

3. Among the brethren there were only two elders who went out and fetched supplies for them. These supervised the tasks performed by each monk. The elder who was permanently employed at the gate told us that the monks within the walls were such saints that all could work miracles and none of them ever fell ill before he died. On the contrary, when the time came for each to depart, he announced it beforehand to all the others and then lay down and fell asleep.

XVIII ON SARAPION

1. In the district of Arsinoë we also visited a priest named Sarapion,[1] the father of many hermitages and the superior of an enormous community numbering about ten thousand monks. Thanks to the labours of the community he successfully administered a considerable rural economy, for at harvest time all of them came as a body and brought him their own produce, which each had obtained as his harvest wage, filling each year twelve *artabas*,[2] or about forty *modii*, as we would say. Through Sarapion they provided this grain for the relief of the poor, so that there was nobody in that district who was destitute any longer. Indeed, grain was even sent to the poor of Alexandria.

2. As a matter of fact, none of the fathers whom we have already mentioned throughout Egypt ever neglected this form of stewardship. On the contrary, from the labours of the brethren they dispatch whole ship-loads of wheat and clothing to Alexandria for the poor, because it is rare for anyone in need to be found living near the monasteries.

3. In the district surrounding Babylon and Memphis I also visited many great fathers and a countless host of monks endowed with every kind of virtue. I also saw Joseph's granaries, where he stored grain in biblical times.[3]

1. There was a monk called Apollonius.[1] The many miracles which he did demonstrated the sanctity of his life. He was honoured with the title of deacon and in every virtue surpassed even the most celebrated monks who have ever lived. **2.** During the persecution this father encouraged the confessors of Christ and succeeded in making many of them martyrs. Then he was arrested himself and thrown into prison. The lowest riff-raff among the pagans came to him and taunted him with angry words and blasphemies.

3. One of these was a flute player, a man famous for his debaucheries. He came to insult him, calling him impious, an impostor and a charlatan, a man hated by everyone and deserving a speedy death. Apollonius said to him, 'May the Lord have mercy on you, my friend, and not count anything you have said as a sin.' When he heard these words, that flute player, who was called Philemon, began to be tortured inwardly, having been pierced by compunction by what the saint had said. **4.** At once he rushed to the tribunal and presented himself to the judge. Moreover, he said to him in front of all the people, 'You are acting unjustly, judge, in punishing innocent men who love God. The Christians neither do anything wrong nor speak any evil; on the contrary they even bless their enemies.'

5. While he was saying this, the judge thought at first that he was joking and being sarcastic. But when he saw that he was serious, he said to him, 'You have gone mad, sir; you have suddenly taken leave of your senses.' But the flute player said, 'I am not mad, you unjust judge; I am a Christian.' The judge, together with the crowd, tried to dissuade him with flattery. But when he saw that he would not change his mind, he subjected him to every kind of torture. **6.** He also had Apollonius seized and, enveloping him in a mass of torments, tortured him as an impostor. But Apollonius said to him, 'I have prayed that you too, judge, and all who are here with you may follow this fraudulent religion of mine.' **7.** On hearing this, the judge ordered both of them to be burnt alive in front of all the people. When the flames were licking round them as the judge looked on, the blessed Apollonius cried out to God in the hearing of all the people and the judge, 'Deliver not to the wild beasts, Master, the soul that confesses thee, (cf. Ps. 74.19) but show thyself clearly to us.' **8.** At this point a cloud like a luminous dewy mist descended and enveloped the men, extinguishing the fire. The crowd and the judge were astounded and cried out, 'There is one God, the God of the Christians.'

9. Some malicious person, however, informed the Prefect of Alexandria what had happened. He sent a detachment of bloodthirsty and ferocious guards and police officers[2] to bring back the judge and Philemon in chains and all who were with them. They also brought Apollonius and some other confessors. 10. While they were all marching along the road, a special grace descended on Apollonius and he began to teach the soldiers. And since they, too, were touched by compunction and believed in the Saviour, they all went to the tribunal in a body chained up together. When the Prefect saw that they were all steadfast in confessing their faith, he ordered them to be thrown into the sea without further delay. But they took this as a symbol of Baptism.

11. When their relations found their bodies washed up on the beach, they buried them in a common grave. There they worked many miracles as they still do to this day. For the saint had acquired such favour with God that whatever he asked for in prayer was at once granted; that is how he was rewarded by the Saviour.

12. We saw him ourselves with his fellow martyrs in the *martyrium*[3] and prayed there. And having worshipped God, we venerated their relics in the Thebaid.

XX ON DIOSCORUS

1. We visited another priest in the Thebaid called Dioscorus,[1] the father of a hundred monks. He used to say to those who were intending to approach the grace of God, 'Take care that no one who has pondered on the image of a woman during the night dare to approach the sacred Mysteries, in case any of you has had a dream while entertaining such an image. 2. 'For seminal emissions do take place unconsciously without the stimulus of imagined forms, occurring not from deliberate choice but involuntarily. They arise naturally and flow forth from an excess of matter. They are therefore not to be classed as sinful. But imaginings are the result of deliberate choice and are a sign of an evil disposition.

3. 'Now a monk,' he said, 'must even transcend the law of nature and must certainly not fall into the slightest pollution of the flesh. On the contrary, he must mortify the flesh and not allow an excess of seminal fluid to accumulate. We should therefore try to keep the fluid depleted by the prolongation of fasting. Otherwise, it arouses our sensual appetites.

4. 'A monk must have nothing whatever to do with the sensual appetites. Otherwise how would he differ from men living in the world? We often see laymen abstaining from pleasures for the sake of their health or for some other rational motive. How much more should the monk take care of the health of his soul and his mind and his spirit.'[2]

ON THE MONKS OF NITRIA

5. We also put in at Nitria,[3] where we saw many great anchorites. Some of them were natives of that region, others were foreigners. They excelled each other in the virtues and engaged in rivalry over their ascetic practices, giving proof of all the virtues and struggling to surpass each other in their manner of life. 6. Some applied themselves to contemplation, others to the active life. When a group of them saw us approaching from a distance through the desert, some came to meet us with water, others washed our feet, and others laundered our clothes. Some of them invited us to a meal, others to learn about the virtues, and others to contemplation and the knowledge of God. Whatever ability each one had, he hastened to use it for our benefit. Indeed how can one relate all their virtues, since one is totally unable to do them justice?

7. They inhabit a desert place and have their cells some distance from each other, so that no one should be recognised from afar by another, or be seen easily, or hear another's voice. On the contrary, they live in profound silence, each monk isolated on his own. They come together in the churches only on Saturdays and Sundays, and meet one another.⁴ Many of them who die in their cells are often not found for four days, because they do not see each other except at the *Synaxis*. 8. Some of them, living as they do so far apart from each other, travel three or four miles to the *Synaxis*. They have so much love for each other, and for other monks too, that when, as often happens, many come desiring to attain salvation by joining them, each one hastens to give them his own hermitage as a temporary cell.

9. I also visited one of the fathers there called Ammonius,⁵ who pos׳ sessed beautifully constructed cells⁶ with a courtyard, a well, and other necessary things. Once a brother came to him, eager to attain salvation. He asked Ammonius to assign him a cell to live in, whereupon the father at once went out, ordering the brother not to leave the cells until he should find him suitable accommodation. And leaving him all he had, together with the cells themselves, he immured himself in a small cell some distance away.

10. If there were many who came to him wishing to be saved, he called together the whole community, and giving bricks to one, and water to another, completed the new cells in a single day. 11. Those who intended to live in the cells were invited to the church for a feast. And while they were still enjoying themselves, each brother filled his cloak or his basket with loaves or other suitable things from his own cell and brought them to the new ones, so that no one should know which gifts had been brought by which brother. When those who were to live in the cells returned to them in the evening, they were surprised to find everything that they needed.

12. We saw there a father called Didymus,⁷ a man of advanced years with a charming countenance. He used to kill scorpions, horned vipers and asps with his bare feet. Nobody else dared do this. Many others who thought they could do the same were killed by the creatures as soon as they touched them.

13. We also saw another father of monks called Cronides,⁸ who had reached a tremendous age. He was a hundred and ten years old, having been one of Antony's original companions. He delivered many admonitions and spiritual discourses to us, but such was the humility which he had guarded right into old age that he considered himself a nonentity.

14. We also saw three brothers who were very fine men. Because of their virtuous way of life they were under compulsion to become bishops. Their

great piety, however, drove them to cut off their ears. This was a very daring thing that they did—although their motive was good—so that no one should bother them in the future.[9]

15. We also visited Evagrius,[10] a wise and learned man who was skilled in the discernment of thoughts, an ability he had acquired by experience. He often went down to Alexandria and refuted the pagan philosophers in disputations.[11] 16. This father exhorted the brothers who were with us not to satiate themselves with water. 'For the demons,' he said, 'frequently light on well-watered places,' He taught us much else about *ascesis*, strengthening our souls.

17. Many of them ate neither bread nor fruit but only endives. Some of them never slept at night, but either sitting or standing persevered in prayer until morning.

1. Many of the fathers who lived there told us about the life of Macarius,[1] the disciple of Antony, who had only just died. Like Antony, he had performed so many miracles and cures and works of power that one could not possibly describe them all. However, we shall record a few of his achievements, relating them briefly.

2. Once he saw some choice palm leaves lying beside Father Antony, with which the great man was working, and asked him for a bundle of them. Antony said to him, 'It is written, "Thou shalt not covet thy neighbour's goods." (Cf. Ex. 20.17; Deut. 5.21.) And as soon as he said this, all the leaves immediately shrivelled up as if they had been parched by fire. On seeing this, Antony said to Macarius, 'See, my spirit has come to rest on you, and you will now be the heir to my virtues.'

3. Some time after this, the devil found Macarius in the desert physically exhausted and said to him, 'Look, you have received the grace of Antony. Why not use this privilege and ask God for food and strength for your journey?' Macarius replied, ' "The Lord is my strength and my song." (Ps. 118.14) As for you, you shall not tempt the servant of God.' 4. The devil then conjured up a mirage for him, a baggage camel lost in the desert and laden with all kinds of useful provisions. When she saw Macarius she came and couched in front of him. But realising that this was a phantasm, which indeed it was, he began to pray. And immediately the camel was swallowed up into the ground.

5. Another time after much fasting and prayer he asked God to show him the paradise which Jannes and Jambres[2] had planted in the desert in their desire to make a copy of the true paradise. 6. When he had wandered through the desert for three weeks, and not having eaten during this time was already fainting, an angel set him near the place. There were demons everywhere guarding the entrances of the paradise and not allowing him to enter. The garden was very large, covering an enormous area. 7. After he had prayed he made a bold effort and succeeded in entering. Inside the garden he found two holy men. They had entered by the same means themselves, and had already spent a considerable time there. When they had said a prayer, they embraced each other, overjoyed at the meeting. Then they washed his feet and set before him some of the fruit of paradise. He partook and gave thanks to God, marvelling at the size of the fruit and

its varied colours. And they said to each other, 'How good it would be if all the monks were here.' **8.** 'In the middle of the paradise,' he said, 'there were three large springs which welled up from the depths and watered the garden and its huge trees, which were very productive and bore every kind of fruit that exists under the heavens.'

9. When he had stayed with them for seven days, Macarius asked if he could go back to the settled region and bring the monks with him. But those holy men said to him that he could not do this. For the desert was a vast trackless waste, and there were many demons in every part of it who made monks lose their way and destroyed them, so that many others who had often wished to come had perished. **10.** But Macarius could not bear to remain here any longer and said, 'I must bring them here that they might enjoy this delight.' He set off in haste for the settled region, carrying some of the fruit as proof. And taking with him a large bundle of palm branches, he planted them as markers in the desert so that he should not lose his way when he came back. **11.** Then he slept for a while in the desert, and when he woke up he found that all the palm branches had been gathered up by the demons and placed by his head. Then getting up, he said to them, 'If it is the will of God, you cannot prevent us from entering into the garden.'

12. When he arrived at the settled region, he kept showing the fruit to the monks to persuade them to come away to the paradise. Many fathers gathered round him and said to him, 'Could it not be that this paradise has come into being for the destruction of our souls? For if we were to enjoy it in this life, we should have received our portion of good things while still on earth. What reward would we have afterwards when we come into the presence of God? For what kind of virtue shall we be recompensed?' And they persuaded Macarius not to return.

13. Another time he was sent some fresh grapes. He desired to eat them, but showing self-control, he sent them to a certain brother who was ill and who was himself fond of grapes. When the brother received them he was delighted, but wishing to conceal his self-mastery, he sent them to another brother, pretending that he had no appetite for any food. When the next brother received the grapes he did the same in turn, although he too had a great desire to eat them.

14. When at length the grapes had been passed round a large number of the brethren without any of them deciding to eat them, the last one to receive them sent them again to Macarius, thinking that he was giving him a rich gift. Macarius recognised them and after inquiring closely into what had happened, marvelled, giving thanks to the Lord for such self-control among the brethren. And in the end not even he partook of the grapes.

15. Another time, they say, Macarius was praying in his cave in the desert. There happened to be another cave nearby which was the den of a hyena. While he was at prayer the hyena suddenly appeared and began to lick his feet. And taking him gently by the hem of his tunic, she drew him towards her own cave. He followed her saying, 'I wonder what this animal wants to do?' **16.** When she had led him to her own cave, she went in and brought out to him her own cubs, which had been born blind. He prayed over them and returned them to the hyena with their sight healed. She in turn, by way of a thank-offering, brought the man the huge skin of a large ram and laid it at his feet. He smiled at her as if at a kind and sensitive person, and taking the skin, spread it under him. This skin is still in the possession of one of the brothers.[3]

17. They also tell the following story of him. A certain evildoer had by magic arts transformed a girl who had consecrated her virginity into a mare. Her parents brought her to him and begged him, if he would be so kind, to change her back into a woman by his prayers. Accordingly, he shut her up on her own for seven days, her parents staying nearby, while he occupied himself with prayer in another cell. On the seventh day he went in with her parents and rubbed her all over with oil. Then he bent his knees and prayed with them, and when they got up they found her transformed back into a young girl.[4]

XXII ON AMOUN

1. Before Macarius there was a Nitrian monk called Amoun,[1] whose soul Antony saw borne up to heaven. He was the first of the monks to settle in Nitria. He was of noble birth and had rich parents, who forced him to marry against his will. When they had compelled him to do this, he persuaded the girl in the bridal chamber that they should both preserve their virginity in secret. **2.** A few days later he departed for Nitria, while she for her part exhorted all her servants to adopt the celibate life, and indeed converted her house into a monastery.[2]

3. Now when he was living as a solitary in Nitria, a child suffering from rabies was brought to him, bound with a chain. For a rabid dog had bitten him and given him the disease. His suffering was so unbearable that his whole body was convulsed by it. **4.** When Amoun saw the child's parents coming to entreat him, he said, 'Why are you troubling me, my friends, seeking something which is beyond my merits, when the remedy lies in your own hands? Give back to the widow the ox which you have killed surreptitiously, and your child will be restored to you in good health.' Their crime having thus been exposed, they happily did what they had been told; and when the father prayed, the child instantly recovered.

5. Another time some people came to visit him. To test their inward dispositions the saint said to them, 'Bring me a storage jar that I may have an ample supply of water for the reception of visitors.' They promised to bring him a jar, but when they came to the village[3] one of them changed his mind and said to the other, 'I am not going to kill my camel; she would die if I loaded a storage jar onto her.' **6.** The other, when he heard this, yoked his asses together and with much labour transported the jar. Before he could speak Amoun said, 'What has happened that your companion's camel has died, while you have made your way here?' When the man returned, he found that the camel had been devoured by wolves.

7. The saint did many other miracles in the sight of all. Once some monks were sent to him by Antony to fetch him. For Antony was in the further desert. When they were on their way back they came to a branch of the Nile. The brothers suddenly saw Amoun transported to the opposite bank, but they themselves crossed over by swimming. **8.** When they came to where Antony was, he spoke first to Amoun, saying, 'God has revealed to me many things concerning you, and he has manifested your departure from this life. I therefore felt compelled to summon you to me that we might enjoy each other's company and intercede for each other.' **9.** Then he set him at a spot some distance away and ordered him not to leave it until he departed this life. When he died, completely alone, Antony saw his soul borne up to heaven by angels.

XXIII ON MACARIUS OF ALEXANDRIA

1. They say that there was another Macarius[1] who was the first to build a hermitage in Scetis.[2] This place is a waste land lying at a distance of a day's and a night's journey from Nitria through the desert. It is a very perilous journey for travellers. For if one makes even a small error, one can get lost in the desert and find one's life in danger. All the monks there have attained perfection. Indeed, no one beset with imperfections could stay in that place, since it is rugged and inhospitable, lacking all the necessities of life.

2. Now this Macarius whom I have mentioned, who was a native of the capital city, one day met with the great Macarius. As they both had to cross the Nile, it so happened that they boarded a very large ferry which two tribunes had also boarded with much commotion. They had a chariot covered entirely in bronze, and horses with gold bridles, and a military escort, and servants apparelled in collars and gold cinctures. 3. When the tribunes saw the monks sitting in the corner dressed in old rags, they blessed their simplicity of life. One of these tribunes said to them, 'Blessed (*macarioi*) are you who have mocked the world.' 4. Macarius of Alexandria said to him, 'We have mocked the world, but the world mocks you. You should know that you have said this not of your own accord but by prophetic inspiration. For we are both called Macarius.' The tribune, moved to compunction by this remark, went home and took off his uniform, and after a generous distribution of alms chose to live as a monk.

1. There was a disciple of Antony's called Paul,[1] who was surnamed 'the Simple'. He caught his wife in the very act of adultery, and without saying a word to anyone set off into the desert to find Antony. And falling at his knees, he begged him to let him live with him because he wished to be saved. Antony said to him, 'You can be saved if you have obedience; whatever I tell you, that is what you will do.' Paul replied, 'I shall do everything you command.' **2.** To test his inward disposition Antony said to him, 'Stand on this spot and pray while I go in and fetch some work for you to do.' He went into the cave and watched Paul through the window. The latter remained motionless on that spot the whole week, roasting in the sun.

3. At the end of the week he came out and said to him, 'Come and have something to eat.' When he had prepared the table and set out the food, he said, 'Sit down and do not eat until the evening; simply keep watch over the dishes.' **4.** When it was evening and Paul had still not eaten, Antony said to him, 'Get up and pray and then lie down and sleep.' Leaving the table, Paul did as he was told. At midnight Antony woke him up for prayer and prolonged the prayers until the ninth hour of the day. He then set the table and again ordered him to eat. **5.** As Paul was about to take his third morsel of bread, Antony commanded him to get up without touching any water, and sent him out to wander in the desert, saying to him, 'Come back after three days.'

6. After he had returned, some brothers came to visit Antony. Paul watched the father to see what tasks he would set him. Antony said to him, 'Serve the brethren in silence and do not taste anything until the brethren have resumed their journey.' **7.** When they had stayed a full three weeks without Paul's having eaten anything, the brethren asked him why he kept silent. When he did not reply, Antony said to him, 'Why are you silent? Speak to the brothers.' And he spoke to them.

8. Another time, when he had brought Antony a jar of honey, the father said, 'Break the jar and pour out the honey.' He did so. Then he said to him, 'Gather up the honey again with a spoon without collecting any dirt with it.' **9.** And again, he ordered him to draw water the whole day. He taught him to weave baskets, and some days later ordered him to undo them all. He unstitched his cloak and ordered him to sew it up again. Again he unstitched it and again Paul sewed it up. 10. And the disciple acquired such absolute obedience that God gave him the grace to drive out demons. Indeed, those demons which Antony was unable to exorcise he sent to Paul, who drove them out instantly.

obedience.

XXV ON PIAMMONAS

1. There is another desert in Egypt close to the sea but very harsh and cruel, where many great anchorites live. It is near Diolcopolis.[1]

2. We saw a priest there called Piammonas,[2] a holy and very humble man who frequently saw visions. Once when he was celebrating the Euchar-ist he saw an angel standing to the right of the altar. The angel was noting the brethren who came up for Communion and writing down their names in a book.[3] As for those who were not present at the *Synaxis,* he saw their names erased. And in fact thirteen days later these died.[4]

3. The demons often tormented this father and made him so weak that he could not stand at the altar or offer the sacrifice. But an angel came, and taking him by the hand, filled him at once with strength and set him at the altar in good health. When the brethren saw the marks of the tortures, they were amazed.

XXVI ON JOHN

We also visited another John[1] in Diolcos, who was the father of hermit/ ages. He, too, was endowed with much grace. He looked like Abraham and had a beard like Aaron's. He had performed many miracles and cures, and was especially successful at healing people afflicted with paralysis and gout.

EPILOGUE

1. We also saw many other monks and fathers throughout Egypt who performed many signs and wonders. Because of their great number we have not mentioned them all. Instead, we have selected a few to represent the many. What should one say about the Upper Thebaid in the district of Syene, where even more wonderful men are to be found and an infinite number of monks? One would not believe their ascetic practices, which surpass human capabilities. 2. To this day they raise the dead and walk on the water just like Peter. And all that the Saviour did through the saints, he does in our own times through these monks.

3. However, as we would have been in the greatest danger if we had gone up beyond Lyco, because of attacks by brigands, we did not dare to visit these saints. As a matter of fact, it was not without danger or hardship that we visited those fathers whom we have mentioned. Nor was it without considerable effort that we saw what is reported in this work. On the contrary, we suffered much on our journey and came very near to losing our lives before we were counted worthy to see these things. Indeed, we came face to face with death seven times, and 'the eighth time no evil touched us'. (cf. Job 5.19)

4. The first time we almost fainted with hunger and thirst after spending five days and five nights walking through the desert.

5. The second time we blundered into some marshy ground full of thorns and prickles, and our feet were so lacerated that the pain became unbearable and we almost perished.

6. The third time we sank into a swamp right up to our waists, 'and there was no deliverer,' (Judges 18.28) and we called out in the words of David, 'Save me O God, for the waters are come in unto my soul. I sink in deep mire, where there is no standing. Deliver me out of the mire, and let me not sink.' (Ps. 69.1,2,14)

7. The fourth time a mass of water encircled us because of the rising of the Nile, and for three days we waded through the water, almost sinking under the surface in the pot-holes. Whenever this happened, we cried out, saying, 'Let not the water-flood overflow me, neither let the deep swallow me up, and let not the pit shut her mouth upon me.' (Ps. 69.15)

8. The fifth time we ran into robbers as we were making our way along the shore to Diolcos. They pursued us so hard in their desire to capture us

that there was scarcely any breath left in our nostrils; indeed, they chased us for about ten miles.

9. The sixth time we were in a boat on the Nile when it capsized and we were nearly drowned.

10. The seventh time we were on Lake Mareotis,[1] where papyrus comes from, when we ran aground on a small desert island. We remained in the open for three days and three nights with rain and a heavy hail-storm beating down on us. For it was the season of Epiphany.[2]

11. As for the eighth time, the story is superfluous but nevertheless profit-able. On our way to Nitria we passed by a certain place where there was a hollow in the land full of water. A number of crocodiles had been stranded there when the floodwaters receded from the surrounding countryside.

12. There were three great crocodiles stretched out on the edge of the pool and we went up to look at the beasts, thinking that they were dead.

13. Suddenly they lunged at us. We called on Christ with a loud voice, crying, 'Christ, help!' The beasts, as if turned aside by some angel, darted into the water. We set off for Nitria at a run without stopping, meditating on the words of Job, where he says, 'He shall deliver thee seven times from tribulations, and in the eighth time no evil shall touch thee.' (cf. Job 5.19)

14. We therefore give thanks to the Lord for delivering us from such great dangers and for showing us such wonderful sights. To him be glory for all eternity. Amen.

NOTES ON THE TEXT

1. *the foundation (hupothesin)* is the practical way of life which enables 'knowledge' *(gnōsin)*, or the direct apprehension of God by the intellect, to be attained.

2. *an exposition (huphēgēsin)*, i.e. the teaching of the fathers who were visited.

3. *the way of virtue (enaretou politeias)*. *Politeia* meant originally the condition of a citizen or the government of a state. It came to mean any organized way of life, whether communal or individual, and was applied almost as a technical term to the life of monks (see *PGL* s.v. F.3.c.ii and G). Elsewhere I have translated it as 'way of life' (VIII 17), 'rule of life' (X 2; XI 5), 'observance' (XIII 10), 'practices' (Prol. 2) and 'ascetic virtues' (II 6). Living according to a *politeia* that frees one from the demands of the body makes one even in this life an *ouranopolitēs*, a citizen of heaven (Prol. 5; cf. XIV 22).

4. A *topos* found in all prologues and Lives. For references see Canivet, *Philotheos*, p.156, n. 6.

5. *community*, lit. 'brotherhood' *(adelphotētos)*. 'Brother' is frequently used as a synonym for 'monk', particularly for a monk living in community. The word *koinobion* never occurs in the *HM*, though we do find a *sunoikia* (community) *koinon ton bion echontōn* (sharing a common life) (VIII 18).

6. *Mount of Olives:* a community for men was founded here by Rufinus in about AD 380 alongside the convent for nuns founded by Melania; presumably all seven monks had been drawn from this house.

7. *the edifying lives of these monks (tēs autōn ōpheleias)*. For *ōpheleia* as 'edification' see Festugière, *HM* (Fr), p.5, n.19. But cf. Canivet, *Philotheos*, p.147, n.2, who prefers 'help', 'usefulness'. Elsewhere I have translated *ōpheleia* as 'benefit'. The word 'monk' *(monachos)* has a curious history. In the pagan world *monos* and *monachos* meant 'singular', 'solitary', 'isolated from contact with each other', 'unique in genre'. In the Greek versions of the Bible (though not in the LXX) *monachos* translates *jahid*, 'isolated', 'solitary', 'deprived of company', 'celibate'. The idea of celibacy strongly influenced the subsequent semantic development of the word. When it first appears in Christian writings, in Athanasius and Eusebius of Caesarea, it is applied to an imitator of Christ leading a solitary life, not necessarily in isolation from others, but certainly celibate and free from attachment to worldly things. Thus from the outset in Christian usage *monachos* could mean a solitary in the strict sense or a celibate imitating Christ with others in a community. For an exhaustive study of the term see Françoise-E. Morard, 'Monachos, Moine: Histoire du terme grec jusqu' au 4e siècle', *Freiburger Zeitschrift für Philosophie und Theologie* 20 (1973), pp.332–411.

8. *stillness (hēsuchian):* already a technical term expressing the state of inner tranquillity and silence which follows the victory over the passions. It is a necessary condition for contemplation.

9. *human vessels,* alluding to Rom. 9.23.

10. On the Incarnation as a *topos* in prologues see Festugière, *HM* (Fr), p.6, n.27s.

11. *in the singing of hymns (en humnois).* These are most likely to be psalms. 'Hymn' is a general term which may refer to a poem or a psalm. Rhythmic compositions had certainly been recited in church from earliest times (see Leclercq, 'Hymnes', *DACL* VI 2826–928 for examples, including Coptic ones). In the *HM,* however, the expressions 'hymnody' and 'hymns and prayers' are frequently used to indicate the work of monks and refer to psalmody. The word is used in its narrower sense on three occasions when the hymns of angels are heard (XI 8, XIV 17, 24).

12. This second group, the monks of the Nile valley, is distinguished from the first, the monks of Nitria.

13. *in the desert and in the countryside (en tais erēmois kai en tais chorais).* The *chora* is the cultivated land in the vicinity of a city or town that supplies its needs. The *erēmos* ('desert') is uninhabited land ranging from pasturage to sandy or stony wastes.

14. *hermitages (monastēriois).* The primary meaning of *monastērion* is the dwelling of a solitary. The word was first used by Philo to describe the hermitages of the Jewish sect of Therapeutae on the shores of Lake Mareotis *(On Contemplative Life* III*).* It was introduced into Christian literature by St Athanasius *(Life of St Antony),* who also applied it to the dwelling of a community of monks (see p.123, n.7). I translate the word as 'hermitage' or 'monastery' according to context.

15. The *desert caves* are those in the 'nearer desert' bordering the Nile valley (see p. 125, n.I 12). The *more remote places* are in the open desert beyond.

16. *in ascetic practices (en tois katorthōmasin).* The word *katorthōma,* originally a Stoic term, comes to mean in Christian usage the attainment of some virtue by ascetic effort. It also includes the idea of merit. For the rivalry between monks in asceticism cf. *HM* XI; the rivalry of the ascetics is discussed by Festugière, *HM* (Fr), pp.78, 90–91.

17. Cf. *Rule of St Benedict,* cap. 73, 'this little Rule for beginners'.

I JOHN OF LYCOPOLIS

1. *Lycopolis:* the present day Asyût (Siout) in Upper Egypt on the west bank of the Nile.

2. *Thebaid:* administrative and diocesan district of central Egypt.

3. *John of Lycopolis:* mentioned by other ancient writers, e.g. Palladius, *Lausiac History* c. xxxv; Cassian, *Institutes* IV 23–6, *Conferences* I, 21, 24, 26; Augustine, *De cura pro mortuis gerenda* 17, *De Civitate Dei* V 26, *Apophthegmata Patrum, Alphabetical series,* 'John of Lycopolis'. His feast is kept on March 27th, *Acta SS* VIII 692–9.

4. Theodosius conducted a war against the Goths in 379–82.

5. Theodosius attacked and captured Maximus in 388.

6. *a general (tinos stratēlatou)*. *Stratēlates* is a broad term for a senior military commander, in this case undoubtedly the *dux Thebaidos*, the provincial commander-in-chief, whose duty it would have been to repel any invasion of the Thebaid. Rufinus calls him a *Romanus dux*.

7. *Ethiopians* is a general term for black men. Here they are probably the Blemyes, a Nubian tribe who had made frequent inroads into Egypt: in 407–8 Nitria and Scetis were devasted.

8. *Syene* (Aswân), on the first cataract and military depot for the frontier of the Thebaid.

9. Theodosius I died on 16 January 395 (Socrates, *HE* 25).

10. *this father*, lit. 'the man' *(ho anēr)*.

11. *tribune:* used loosely of any senior legionary officer.

12. *on the desert escarpment*, lit. 'in the mountain' *(en tō orei)*. In Egypt the word *oros* signified both 'mountain' and 'desert'; the Egyptian desert ends abruptly in an escarpment overlooking the flat valley floor of the Nile. *Oros* is therefore barren, uncultivated land, not necessarily rising to any height, as against the irrigated zone of the valley and delta. Five distinct meanings of *oros* may be distinguished: (a) the open desert, also called 'the remoter desert' (I 44) and 'the further desert' (I 45); (b) the desert escarpment, also called 'the nearer desert'; (c) the strip of land between the alluvial plain and the escarpment, marking the extreme limit of cultivated land (also called 'the nearer desert'), which was the situation of numerous Egyptian monasteries. From these usages come two further religious senses: (a) a monastery and (b) a zone where monasteries are concentrated (as in 'the mountain of Nitria', which is in fact flat). See H. Cadell & R. Rémondon, 'Sens et emplois de *to oros* dans les documents papyrologiques', *Revue des Études Grecques* 80 (1967) pp.343–9.

13. *high-ranking officer (praipositou)*. *Praipositos* refers to a post rather than a rank. There were civil *praipositoi* in charge of the administration, but here a military *praipositos* is clearly intended, the commander of a fort or garrison directly responsible to the *dux*.

14. *in the knowledge of God (kat' epistēmēn)*. This is not *gnōsis*, the direct knowledge of God which comes through contemplation, but the biblical knowledge of God *(epistēmē)*, akin to wisdom, which is acquired by learning (cf. Sirach 16.24).

15. The Nile floods between August and November.

16. The Greek cities of Egypt, Alexandria, Naucratis, Ptolemais-Hermiou and Antinoöpolis, had their own senates.

17. *ascesis*. In classical Greek *askēseis* are the exercises of athletes and soldiers (still the primary sense in modern Greek). An 'ascetic' *(askētēs)* was a trained and experienced soldier or athlete. The development of a moral sense enabled the word

to be applied to a man of virtue. *Ascesis* entered the patristic vocabulary through Philo. In imitation of Philo Clement of Alexandria takes the wrestling Jacob as the type of the Christian *askētēs* (*Paed.* 1, 7; *PG* 8, 17). Origen calls *askētai* those who profess the perfect life. In monastic usage *askēsis* comes to mean the struggle to free oneself from the passions by the specific disciplines of continence, fasting and prayer. Occasionally I have translated *askēsis* as 'ascetic discipline'. See M. Viller and M. Olphe-Galliard, 'Ascèse, Ascéticisme' *DS* I 938–77.

18. *a poor man*, lit. 'a humble man', an obligatory *topos* of humility.

19. The *Life of St Antony* was known in Palestine; visitors had also spread rumours of Egyptian monasticism cf. pp.3–4.

20. *a picture (historia)*. *Historia* means primarily 'an investigation' or 'a narrative' (as in the Greek title to this work). In monastic writings it can also mean 'a picture' or a 'representation' (see *PGL* s.v. C 4).

21. One of the reasons given for life in the desert was that the Bible was read in churches in towns and so the devil had been driven into the desert, where he was to be fought.

22. *passion (pathos)*. The passions in classical antiquity were the 'emotions', the movements of the soul which gave rise to the sensations of pleasure or pain. From their first appearance in Christian writings early in the third century they are specifically the disordered impulses of the appetitive aspect of the soul (following the Platonic tripartite division) which need to be controlled by the intelligent aspect. A man who follows these impulses will give in to sin. In the *HM* the passions give the demons a foothold in the soul (XV 2–3). The goal of the struggle against the passions (by means of *ascesis*) is *apatheia*, a stripping away of the passions so that the soul, no longer bothered by impulses towards sin, can come to the direct knowledge of God. For the best modern account of *apatheia* see T. Špidlík, *La spiritualité de l'orient chrétien*, *OCA* 206, Rome, 1978, pp.261–70.

23. *the simulation of priestly virtue (hierateias hupokrisis)*. The phrase is ambiguous. From the fourth century *hierateia* (the priesthood) is used of the Christian episcopate and presbyterate (see *PGL* s.v.). But in the NT it refers solely to the Jewish priesthood (Lk. 1.9; Heb. 7.5). Here John may be warning his hearers against a hypocrisy like that of the Jewish religious leaders, but more probably he is warning them not to aim at the priesthood from unworthy motives, pretending to be suitable candidates.

24. *this knowledge (gnōsin)* refers to 'seeing God' of the previous sentence.

25. *to free the appetites from passion*, lit. 'to acquire *apatheia* with regard to the appetites' (cf. note 22).

26. *And again*: an indication that the author is quoting from a literary source, probably a collection of Apophthegmata of John.

27. It was the custom of pagan ascetics to live in tombs and this was followed by Christian monks (cf. *Life of St Antony* 8). Tombs, like the desert itself, were the

dwelling-places of demons and were therefore sought out by ascetics who wished to do battle with them.

28. For hermits fed by the bread of heaven cf. p.44.

29. *by evil thoughts (tois logismois)*. *Logismoi* are impassioned mental images. The following definition is from Evagrius: 'A demonic *logismos* is an image *(eikōn)* belonging to the sensitive life of a man which has been composed in the under-standing *(kata dianoian)*, with which the mind *(nous)* when moving in an impassioned way says something or does something secretly against the law in accordance with the image *(eidōlon)* which has effected an entrance because the mind has been overpowered by it' (cited by Thomas Špidlík, *La spiritualité de l'orient chrétien*, p.233).

30. Cf. Dioscorus, XXI, p.105.

31. *the inhabited region (tēn oikoumenēn):* i.e. the valley floor of the Nile, as opposed to the *erēmos*, the desert. Occasionally *oikoumenē* is translated as 'the settled region'.

32. *gifts (eulogias)*. The primary meaning of *eulogia* is 'blessing'. The word was applied especially to the bread not needed for consecration in the Eucharist which was blessed separately and distributed at the end of the service. Cenobitic monks consumed it with wine as a collation after the Eucharist. Blessed bread was also sent out as a gift. However, the word could also be used more widely for any gift. Abba Arsenius was given some dried figs as an *eulogia* (*Sayings of the Desert Fathers*, Arsenius 16 [*PG* 65, 92B]). Egeria on her visit to Mount Sinai was given some *eulogiae* which was fruit grown by the monks (*Egeria's Travels* trans. John Wilkinson, London 1971, pp.24–5, 94). *PGL* s.v. E.3 cites this passage from the *HM* as an example of blessed bread sent as a gift, but there is nothing to suggest that *eulogia* here is being used in its narrower sense. In the *HM* the word always occurs in the plural and I translate it consistently as 'gifts'.

33. The theme of 'active works' as a preparation for prayer is frequently discussed in Christian spirituality. Cf. Augustine of Hippo, *De Civitate Dei* viii 4; Gregory the Great, *Homilies on Ezekiel* ii 2, 7–8.

34. Eugenius and Arbogast were defeated and killed by Theodosius in September 394. This mention, together with the reference to the Epiphany (6 January) in the Epilogue, furnishes the date of the journey, the winter of 394–5.

35. The prophecy of the death of Theodosius is repeated here. Cf. p.52.

36. The date thus given for the death of John, late 394 or early 395, fits in with information given by Palladius. Cf. *Lausiac History*, vol. i, pp.181–2, vol. ii, p.213, n.64.

37. This section ends with a doxology and 'amen', perhaps indicating its in-dependent existence before it was included in this work.

II ABBA OR

1. Abba Or is known to us only from this account. There was another Or of Nitria who was already dead when Palladius first went to Nitria in about 390 (cf. *Lausiac History* c. IX). *Abba* was a title of respect given to senior monks. The superior of a monastery or of a community of anchorites is called a father *(patēr)*.

2. *He looked just like an angel (schēma men echonta angelikon)*. PGL cites this *(schēma* 8.c.iv) as meaning 'he wore the angelic schema', (i.e. the monastic habit), a possible meaning but unlikely in the context.

3. *pickled vegetables (lachanois sunthetois):* green vegetables preserved in oil or salt. (See HM (Fr) p.31, n.27s). Their preparation is described by Theodoret: 'They collected vegetables that were growing wild, and putting them in pots, covered them with as much brine as was sufficient, and so had a delicacy for those who needed nursing' *(Philotheos* II 4, pp.200–2). PGL's 'mixed' for *sunthetois,* citing this passage (s.v. I.B.2), is inadequate.

4. *he was able to recite the Scriptures by heart (tas graphas exōthen apestēthizen).* The author of the HM, unlike Palladius, treats this as a miraculous charism (cf. Pater- muthius X 7). Armand Veilleux says that a widespread form of prayer among ancient monks was the meditative recitation of Scripture aloud or *sotto voce—'une sorte de rumination du texte inspiré'.* In his opinion 'even though they forced themselves to learn the greatest possible part of Scripture by heart, and even though meditation is designated in Greek by the verbs *ekstēthizein* or *apostēthizein,* this did not necess- arily imply a recitation from memory' (Veilleux, p.268).

5. *to participate in the Eucharist:* lit. 'to the prayers' *(epi tas euchas).* That this expression signifies the Eucharist is made clear by the context.

6. *a false brother (pseudadelphou tinos):* a Pauline term (cf. 2 Cor. 11.26; Gal. 2.4) which is used here to indicate a man who adopts the monastic life from unworthy motives (for an easy life, or to escape debts, etc.). This monk presumably wished to acquire an additional set of clothing for profit.

III AMMON

1. *Ammon:* several monks of this name are known in Egypt in this period (cf. the list in *Lausiac History* vol. II, p.190, n.16). Others of the same name or variations of it are mentioned in HM IX, XV 2, XX 9, XXII and XXV.

2. *Tabennisiots:* Cenobitic monks who followed the Pachomian Rule were called Tabennisiots after St Pachomius's first monastery at Tabennisi nearly two hun- dred miles upstream from Lycopolis. There were two Pachomian monasteries near Hermopolis Magna (Eshmunên). One of these is likely to have been the monastery of Ammon (cf. *Lausiac History,* vol. II, p.209).

3. *sheepskin cloaks (mēlotas).* The melote, an unshorn sheepskin cloak (from *mēlon,* sheep), was part of the habit of a Pachomian monk and was worn in the refectory

(cf. *Lausiac History*, vol. II, p.89). It was the 'mantle' of Elijah (I Kings 19.13 LXX) and the dress of the prophets in the Letter to the Hebrews who wandered 'in deserts, and in the mountains, and in dens and caves of the earth' (Heb. 11.37–8). Cf. Cassian, *Institutes* I 3.

4. *with their faces veiled (kekalummenō prosōpō):* i.e. with their hoods pulled down low over their faces. Cf. Cassian, *Institutes* IV 17.

5. *soup:* cf. *Rule of St Pachomius* 44.

6. *the edification which may be drawn from this rule of life (tēn ek tautēs tēs politeias ōpheleian).* There are two MS readings here. The **x** family, which Festugière has shown to have priority, reads *tēn ek tautēs ōpheleian.* The larger **y** family has *tēn ek toutōn ōpheleian.* I am convinced by Festugière's explanation of how **y** has emended **x** to normalise the grammar after the loss of a word following *tautēs* (*HM* (Fr) pp.lx–lxi), but I do not accept his emendation, *ek tautēs tēs diēgēseōs* ('from this narrative') which he proposes on analogy with the second paragraph of the Prologue. The author is edified not by his written account, which is not under consideration here, but by the practices and observances of the monks. I have therefore replaced *diēgēseōs* with my own emendation, *politeias* (cf. Prol. n.3).

IV BES

1. *Bes:* not otherwise known.

V OXYRHYNCHUS

1. Very little is known about the history of Oxyrhynchus (Bêhnesa) apart from what can be gleaned from the many papyri discovered there. It was a walled town which profited from the decline of Heracleopolis and became a thriving Christian centre. By about 300 it already had two churches (cf. Kees, Pauly-Wissowa, s.v. Oxyrynchos, cols. 2043 ff.).

2. *the temples and capitols (hoi naoi kai ta kapetolia).* The *naoi* are the former temples of the native Egyptian gods. A *capitolium* in Latin Christian writers was any pagan temple or even a Christian church (Du Cange, *Gloss.*). But it had a more specific meaning which is clearly intended here. Every important city in the Roman Empire had a *capitolium*, a temple of the official cult which housed statues of the Capitoline triad (Jupiter Capitolinus, Fides and Victoria). We know from a papyrus of c. 300 listing the watchmen stationed at public buildings in Oxyrhynchus (Wilcken, *Chrestom.* 474, cf. Milne pp. 235–6) that this city had a *capitolium* and a *Caesareum* (a temple of the divinised Caesars). The plural *kapetolia* either refers loosely to these two Roman temples, or, as Festugière says (*HM* (Fr) p.38, n.6), has become plural by analogy with *hoi naoi.*

3. *oratories (euktēria):* this is the only instance cited in *PGL* for a monastery chapel.

4. *offer acts of worship to God (tas latreias . . . epeteloun tō theō* [cf. Heb. 9.6: *tas latreias epitelountes*]). Elsewhere a similar phrase (*prospheron tō theō . . . tas latreias,* XXV 2)

undoubtedly refers to the Eucharist. Here it must be the Office, as the Eucharist would not have been celebrated at any time of the day or night. The phrase 'no hour of the day or night' is simply an expression to indicate the vast throng of monks. In about 404 Alexander the Sleepless founded a monastery in Constantinople where a continuous cycle of prayer was kept up throughout the twenty four hours of the day and night. If such a régime had existed in Oxyrhynchus, however, it would surely have excited more detailed comment.

5. *bless (dounai . . . eirēnēn):* lit. 'to give peace'. By the fourth century *eirēnē pasin* (peace to all) was already the bishop's greeting in the Liturgy.

6. *the chief officials and magistrates (hoi de stratēgoi autōn kai hoi archontes).* The *stratēgos* was the governor of a nome, the next unit of administration below the province (which was under an *epistratēgos*). His duties included the farming and collection of taxes and the command of the police. Sometimes a nome had two *stratēgoi*, but the plural here may simply be by analogy with *archontes* (cf. *kapetolia*, n.2). The *archontes* were the body of magistrates which Augustus had established in each metropolis for the supervision of the gymnasium, ephebic training, the Greek temples, the market and the corn supply.

7. *agora:* the market place used for debates as well as trade.

VI THEON

1. *the city:* Oxyrhynchus.

2. Theon is known only from this account.

VII ELIAS

1. *Antinoë* = Antinoöpolis (Shêkh 'Abâda), a city in Middle Egypt on the east bank of the Nile, founded by Hadrian in AD 130 in memory of his favourite, Antinous, who had been drowned while on a journey up the river. It had a Greek constitution modelled on that of Naucratis.

2. A metropolis was the capital of a nome. Antinoë, occupying a strategic position at the head of a road to the Red Sea, was also the administrative centre of the Thebaid.

3. Elias is not otherwise known to us. Another Elias was superior of a large monastery at Atripe near Panopolis in Upper Egypt (*Lausiac History* c. XXIX).

VIII APOLLO

1. *Apollo:* born 305/8; withdrew to the desert at the age of fifteen, 320/3; returned at the age of fifty five, 360/3; founded a coenobium at the age of eighty, 385/8. The visit of the seven monks was therefore when he was between eighty six and eighty nine. Since the writer says that Apollo 'would now be a hundred', this may mean that he was writing in 405.

2. *Hermopolis* (Eshmûnên) was on the west bank of the Nile on the border between Middle and Upper Egypt. Goods passing up and down the Nile paid customs dues there.

3. On the flight into Egypt cf. the apocryphal *Gospel of Matthew* 22–3 and Sozomen, *HE* V 21 (*PG* 67.128).

4. *in the desert at the foot of the mountain:* i.e. the strip of arid land between the valley floor and the escarpment.

5. *great monastery:* the ruins have been discovered and excavated at Bawit, about fifteen miles south of Hermopolis (See Festugière *HM* (Fr) p.63, n.390ss).

6. Julian the Apostate, 361–3.

7. *a tunic (ho lebitōn):* lit. 'the leviton'. The two instances of this word in the *HM* are the only citings in *PGL*, but we know what it was from Jerome's Latin version of the *Rule of St Pachomius* (No. 2): 'a linen tunic without sleeves [or cuffs] which they call a levitonarium'. *Colobium* (from *kolobos*, cut short) was the name which Cassian adopted for the monastic tunic (*Institutes* I). The sleeves of his tunic came down to the elbows.

8. Conscription of monks for military service was instituted under Valentinian and Valens, because of the numbers who evaded service by claiming to be monks.

9. Cf. Eusebius *HE* V.

10. Cf. John of Lycopolis *HM* I 11.

11. *a pagan:* lit. 'a Hellene'.

12. *assisted at the Eucharist and received Communion:* lit. 'communicated from the Eucharist of Christ'.

13. Cf. Cassian, *Institutes* V 1 on the sin of *tristitia*.

14. This quotation is not scriptural but from the *Life of St Antony*. Rufinus replaces it with Matt. 25.35.

15. The 69th of the *Apostolic Canons* (fourth cent.) prescribes fasting in Lent and on Wednesdays and Fridays on pain of deposition for clerics and excommunication for laymen (Pitra I p.29). Already in the Didache (second cent.), however, Wednesdays and Fridays are laid down as fast days (*Didache* VIII). The reasons given by Apollo for keeping these days reflect a passage from Peter of Alexandria's Paschal Letter for 306 (appended to his Fourteen Canons on Penance): 'Let no one reproach us for keeping every Wednesday and Friday, for it is reasonably prescribed according to tradition that we should fast on these days: Wednesday because that is when the Jews held their council for the betrayal of the Lord, and Friday because that is when he suffered for us.' (Pitra I p.561)

16. The wearing of chains as an ascetic practice seems to have been more common in Syria, where greater austerities were practised, than in Egypt (cf. *Lausiac History*, vol I, p.241; vol. II, p.215, n.69, p.221, n.81). Theodosius of Rhosos is a good example of the kind of ascetic censured by Apollo: 'He added to these practices the loading of

a mass of iron on his neck, and loins, and both his wrists; and he wore his hair matted and tumbling down to his feet, and even flowing beyond them, and for this reason kept it tied round his waist' (*Philotheos* X 2, p.438).

17. *human approbation (anthrōpareskeian):* the Pauline 'men-pleasing' (cf. Eph. 6.6).

IX AMOUN

1. *a large serpent (megalou drakontos):* lit. 'a large dragon' (cf. Rev. 12.3–9). Before the rise of monasticism 'dragon' was simply a name for the devil ('What corporeal dragon has ever been described as having been seen in the corporeal river of Egypt,' says Origen [*PG* 14, 284B]). Athanasius calls 'the dragon' the devil who fights Antony in various forms. In the *HM* the dragon becomes a real serpent. Cf. Theodoret, *Philotheos* III 7, where the dragon also bursts.

2. This monster was twenty-two feet long at a conservative estimate. The cubit varied between eighteen and twenty-two inches.

3. *Amoun:* a hermit of the Thebaid; not otherwise known.

4. Rev. 20.1–3.

X COPRES

1. *priest (presbuteros).Presbuteros* (the comparative of *presbus,* old) had by the fourth century become the technical term for the order of ministry between bishop and deacon. However, it also continued to be used in its older and vaguer sense of a venerable old man. I have therefore translated it as 'elder' or as 'priest' according to context.

2. *Copres,* a priest and superior of a monastery. Another Copres is mentioned as a member of the crew of the Tabennisiot boat which was a ferry on the Nile. There was also an Abba Copres of Scetis (*Sayings of the Desert Fathers,* Copres).

3. *superior (hēgoumenos).* By the mid-fifth century this was the technical term for the head of a cenobitic monastery. In the fourth century it was still used as a general term for anyone exercising civil or ecclesiastical authority. It is the only instance of the term in the *HM.*

4. Patermuthius is known only from this account. He seems to have been regarded as the founder of the monastic group here; a wanderer, like many early monks, Copres attaches exaggerated legends to his name.

5. This anchoress is presented as living in a small house, probably with two rooms, alone, but near to a community of priests with a church.

6. *the inner chamber (to tamieion).* This is the 'closet' of Matt. 6.6 to which we are urged to retire to pray. But the word also means a treasury or store-room, and it was no doubt as such that it was object of Patermuthius's attempted burglary.

7. *baptized him (phōtisantes auton):* lit. 'illuminated him'. From the early second

century 'to illuminate' was synonymous with 'to baptize', and included a reference to the instruction received before the rite. Note that here Patermuthius's baptism follows his years in the desert and his knowledge of the Scriptures.

8. The teaching role of the monks as missionaries to their pagan neighbours is here mentioned, a rare instance.

9. The religion of Mani (216–77) spread from Persia to Egypt in the late third century.

XI SOUROUS

1. *Sourous:* a disciple of Pachomius of this name is mentioned in the *Sayings of the Desert Fathers*, Psenthaisios.

2. *Isaiah:* there was a monk of this name at Nitria (*Lausiac History* c. XIV).

3. *Paul:* a familiar name in the desert; cf. *HM* XXIV.

4. *Anouph:* not otherwise known; an ascetic of local fame. The story is a fable to illustrate virtues, and the characters mentioned cannot therefore be identified.

XII HELLE

1. *Helle:* known only from this account.

2. *Synaxis.* Etymologically *synaxis* means 'a meeting' or 'a collection'. In monastic writings it can mean any meeting in church for the office or the Eucharist (sometimes even the church itself) or a collection of prayers which a monk has adopted as his *politeia*. The precise meaning can only be determined from the context. In the *HM*, however, it always seems to mean the Eucharist (cf. Veilleux, pp.229–35, 293–4).

XIII APELLES

1. *Achoris* (Tehna): on the east bank of the Nile in Middle Egypt.

2. *Apelles:* a priest known only from this source, who had been a blacksmith.

3. *John* the Hermit, not John of Lycopolis; he seems to have followed the early traditions of the desert in asceticism.

4. The priest was link-man and interpreter for the illiterate hermit.

XIV PAPHNUTIUS

1. *Paphnutius:* several monks were known by this name in Egypt; cf. Cassian, *Conferences* XVIII 15; *Sayings of the Desert Fathers*, Paphnutius; *Lausiac History* c. XLVI. This Paphnutius is described as a hermit near Heracleopolis in the Fayyum.

2. A player of the tibia, a reed instrument with two pipes joined at the mouth; it was used in pagan ceremonies and connected by the Christians with debauchery.

3. *by agents of the governor and the city councillors (hupo tōn taxeōtōn tou archontos kai tōn bouleutōn).* The *archōn* (ruler) was no doubt the *stratēgos* of the nome who had the power to enforce the collection of taxes. The 'agents' *(taxeōtai)* were the apparitors attached to all functionaries who had an official salaried post (*taxis*) (see L. Robert, *Hellenica* XI/XII, p.50). Each metropolis had a council *(boulē)* which appointed the magistrates and more important officials of the nome below the rank of *stratēgos.*

4. *arrears of taxes (chreos dēmosion):* lit. 'a public debt'. No doubt the husband was a *praktōr* (an unpaid tax farmer) who had failed to raise the sum assigned to him by the *stratēgos* and was therefore personally responsible for the amount by which he fell short (cf. Milne, pp. 137–8).

5. *gold coins (chrusinōn):* solidi, or *nomismata,* as they were often called in Egypt. Since the monetary reforms of Diocletian the gold *solidus* had provided the standard for accountancy in Egypt (cf. Milne, pp.262–3).

6. *a merchant of Alexandria:* who travelled along the Nile trading in beans; cf. W. Willcocks, *Egyptian Irrigation,* London, 1889, for growth of beans and lentils in the Nile delta.

XV PITYRION

1. Pispir (Der-el-Memun), the 'Outer Mountain' of St Antony; cf. *Lausiac History,* vol. II, p.199, n.37.

2. *Pityrion:* a disciple of St Antony the Great and successor to Ammonas by 394 at Pispir, though Rufinus does not mention him there in 373.

3. *Ammonas:* a disciple of St Antony and author of the *Letters of Ammonas.*

XVI EULOGIUS

1. *Eulogius:* a priest; there were others of the same name; cf. *Lausiac History* c. XXI.

2. Cf. XX Dioscorus and note.

3. Doubts about the Eucharist were also expressed elsewhere in this literature; cf. *Sayings of the Desert Fathers,* Daniel 7.

4. *the grace of God:* i.e. Communion.

XVII ISIDORE

1. *Isidore:* a familiar name in the Thebaid. Butler identifies six monks called Isidore (*Lausiac History,* vol. II, p. 185, n. 7). This one was the head of a large monastery with particularly rigid rules about enclosure. There seems to have been no contact here between the visitors and the monks except for the gate-keeper.

XVIII SARAPION

1. *Sarapion:* several monks were called by this name in the desert. The body of a 'Sarapion' was found at Antinoë, buried with penitential chains round it (cf. *Lausiac History,* vol. II, pp.213–6, nn.68–9).

2. *artabas:* the *artabē* was an 'Egyptian measure of capacity varying from 24 to 42 *choinikes'* (*LSJ* s.v. II). The normal wage for a labourer was based on an allowance of two to three *artabas* a month (Milne, p.257). Twelve *artabas* would therefore represent one man's harvest wage. As the *artabē* varied from place to place, the amount in standard Roman *modii* is given, which is equivalent to ten bushels (350 litres).

3. Presumably the 'granaries of Joseph' were the pyramids (cf. Rufinus, *HM* c. XVIII).

XIX APOLLONIUS

1. *Apollonius:* a deacon in the Thebaid. The martyrology for 10 April (*Acta SS.* IX 862–3) says: 'the holy martyr the priest Apollonius of Alexandria with five others, who were thrown into the sea in the persecution of Maximian (293–310).' This Apollonius seems to have been confused here with Apollonius the martyr of the Thebaid, who is commemorated with his companion Philemon on 8 March (*Acta SS.* VI 751–7).

2. *guards and police officers (protiktoras kai taxeōtas).* The *protiktorai* (= Latin *pro-tectores*) were the body-guard of the Prefect of Alexandria, the supreme governor of the whole diocese of Egypt. For *taxeōtai* see note XIV 3, p.134.

3. *martyrium:* a martyr's shrine. The Greek version of the Acta of Apollonius and Philemon adds after their beheading in Antinoë: 'Devout men then received their bodies and after laying them out in a decent manner deposited them in the place where the relics of SS. Asclas and Leonidas rested.' (*Acta SS.* VI 755C; cf. H. Delehaye, *Les origines du culte des martyrs,* Brussels 1912, p.253).

XX DIOSCORUS

1. *Dioscorus:* a priest and abbot of a monastery, otherwise unknown.

2. For canon law in the East on nocturnal emissions cf. Timothy of Alexandria, *Questions and Answers* (confirmed by the Sixth and Seventh Ecumenical Councils) 12: 'a layman who has suffered a nocturnal emission should not have Communion if this is because he has himself by deliberate choice entertained desire for a woman in his heart. But if the reason is temptation from the demon, then he may have Communion.' Dionysius of Alexandria (third cent.), Canon 3, says the same. John the Faster, Canon 6 (? ninth cent.) is more severe and forbids Communion in all cases. Athanasius, Letter to Ammoun, treats nocturnal emissions as natural excretions, not to be considered as sin. The view Dioscorus takes is that of Timothy

and Dionysius, which may reflect the standard opinion in fourth-century Egypt. (We are indebted to the Archimandrite Kallistos Ware for this note.)

NITRIA

3. Nitria is now properly identified as a flat desert promontory extending northwards into the Delta, forty miles south of Alexandria near a branch of the Nile. It takes its name from the natron (soda) collected there in the ancient world and today; cf. White, pp.17–42.

4. For the tradition of Saturday and Sunday gatherings for liturgical celebration cf. Cassian, *Institutes* II 18, and Veilleux, pp. 234–5, 248.

5. *Ammonius:* one of the four Tall Brothers, the others being Eusebius, Euthymius and Dioscorus, who was already bishop of Hermopolis Parva (Damanhur); cf. Socrates, *HE* VI 7, and *Lausiac History* c. x.

6. *cells:* probably 'the Cells' (Cellia), a quiet retreat founded by Amoun of Nitria about twelve miles south of the Nitrian settlements on the track to Scetis (cf. White, pp.24–5). A. Guillaumont may have excavated this very convent; see A. Guillaumont, 'Les fouilles françaises des Kellia 1964–9' in R. McL. Wilson, *The Future of Coptic Studies*, Leiden 1978, pp.206–7.

7. *Didymus:* obviously not Didymus the Blind (*Lausiac History* c. iv).

8. *Cronides:* a companion of St Antony the Great; cf. *Lausiac History* c. xxi and *Letters of Ammonas* c. xxix.

9. This was also said of Ammonius when Timothy of Alexandria wanted to ordain him in 381. The 22nd Apostolic Canon says that anyone who has mutilated himself may not become a cleric; the 24th Canon sentences a layman who mutilates himself to three years deprivation of Communion (Pitra I p.17). That is why the brothers' deed was very daring.

10. *Evagrius:* he is here highly praised. He was the centre of the Origenist party in Egypt, lived in Nitria, and was the friend of Palladius; cf. *Lausiac History* c. xxxviii. He was born in Pontus in 346, became a disciple of the Macarii, lived in Nitria and the Cells, where Palladius knew him, and died in 399. His writings were once suspected of Origenism; cf. A. and C. Guillaumont, 'Evagre le Pontique' in *DS* IV 1731–44. For his works see the Bibliography.

11. *disputations:* not otherwise known; but as Evagrius had gained a reputation for his dialectical ability in disputations with heretics in Constantinople (*Lausiac History* c. xxxviii), not unlikely.

XXI MACARIUS

1. Macarius the Egyptian: cf. *Lausiac History* c. xiii, *Sayings of the Desert Fathers*, Macarius. He was born in c. 300, became a monk at thirty under St Anthony the Great. He died five years before this visit and one year before Palladius arrived in

Egypt (*Lausiac History* c. LXIX). The stories told of the two Macarii are often confused, as here.

2. *Jannes and Jambres*; cf. Patermuthius, X 21, p.85. These were two Egyptian magicians who imitated the miracles of Moses and planted an earthly paradise; cf. Exod. 7.11–12, 2 Tim. 3.8, Origen, *Commentary on St Matthew, Series* 117. Here a story told of Macarius and two naked saints (*Lausiac History* c. XVIII) is conflated with a story of a visit to paradise usually told of Macarius the Alexandrian.

3. Cf. *Lausiac History* c. XVIII; the sheepskin was said to have been given to Melania as a keepsake after his death.

4. But see the version in Rufinus and the *Lausiac History* c. XVII, where the girl is said to have been the victim of the delusions of others.

XXII AMOUN

1. Amoun of Nitria: *Lausiac History* c. VIII and p.190, n.16.

2. Nuns and convents of nuns are frequently mentioned in the *Lausiac History*: cc. III, VI, XXVIII, XXXIII, XXXIV, XLI, XLVI, LIV, LVII, LIX, LXI, LXIII, LXVII.

3. *the village*: i.e. of Nitria (El Barnugi).

XXIII MACARIUS OF ALEXANDRIA

1. Macarius of Alexandria, or the Citizen: a sweetmeat seller turned monk in Scetis at the age of forty. Born c. 293, he lived for one hundred years. He met Palladius and trained him in Egypt. He had four cells in Nitria, Cellia, Scetis and in the SW; cf. *Lausiac History* c. XVIII. His feast is celebrated on 2 January: *Acta SS*. I 84. The question of the composition of the homilies once attributed to him is still open. A *Life of St Macarius* has recently been translated into French by Dom Michel van Parys (Chevtogne).

2. *Scetis*: the Wadi Natrun, forty miles south of Nitria across the desert; it proved too dangerous for the seven to visit and this account is hearsay; cf. White, pp.17–24.

XXIV PAUL

1. Paul the Simple: cf. *Sayings of the Desert Fathers*, Paul the Simple, and *Lausiac History* c. XXII. There were other monks called Paul (*Lausiac History*, vol. II, p.201, n.40) but this disciple of St Antony the Great is identifiable from his simple-mindedness and severe training, the only instance of such obedience in this text.

XXV PIAMMONAS

1. *Diolcopolis* (= Diolcos), a town on the coast between the Sebennytic and Phatnic mouths of the Nile; cf. Cassian, *Institutes* V 36, *Conferences* XVIII 1.

2. *Piammonas* gave the eighteenth of Cassian's *Conferences*; he was Cassian's first teacher in Egypt.

3. This story was popular later; cf. *Exordium Magnum Cisterciense,* ed. B. Griesser, Rome 1961, Bk. II c. iii pp.100–101 for a similar story of St Bernard of Clairvaux.

4. Presumably this lapse of time had allowed, in vain, for amendment before the next Sunday.

XXVI JOHN

1. Cassian met John at Diolcos and assigns the nineteenth *Conference* to him.

EPILOGUE

1. *Lake Mareotis:* Lake Maryut; cf. *Lausiac History* c. VII. In the fourth century it seems to have been much larger than it is today. For a discussion of the district see A. de Cosson, *Mareotis,* London 1935, esp. c. VII, 'Early Monastic Communities'.

2. *Epiphany:* 6 January; this marks the date of the return journey.

THE ADDITIONS OF RUFINUS

GREEK	LATIN	GREEK	LATIN
Prologue	Prologue		John
1 John of Lyco-	1 John of Lyco-		16 Paphnutius
polis	polis	17 Isidore	17 Isidore
2 Or	2 Or	18 Sarapion	18 Sarapion
3 Ammon	3 Ammon	19 Apollonius	19 Apollonius
4 Bes	4 Bes	20 Dioscorus	20 Dioscorus
5 Oxyrhynchus	5 Oxyrhynchus	Nitria	21 Nitria
6 Theon	6 Theon		22 Cellia
7 Elias		(Ammonius)	23 Ammonius
8 Apollo	7 Apollo	(Didymus)	24 Didymus
9 Amoun	8 Amoun	(Cronides)	25 Cronius
10 Copres	9 Copres		26 Origenes
Patermuthius	Patermuthius	(Evagrius)	27 Evagrius
11 Sourous	10 Sourous	21 Macarius	28 Macarii
12 Helle	11 Helle	22 Amoun	
	12 Elias	23 Macarius of	29 Macarius of
13 Apelles		Alexandria	Alexandria
John			30 Amoun
14 Paphnutius		24 Paul	31 Paul
15 Pityrion	13 Pityrion	25 Piammonas	32 Piammonas
16 Eulogius	14 Eulogius	26 John	33 John
	15 Apelles	Epilogue	Epilogue

A COMPARATIVE TABLE OF CHAPTERS IN THE GREEK AND
LATIN VERSIONS OF THE HISTORIA MONACHORUM

THE ADDITIONS OF RUFINUS

There are a number of differences between the text of Rufinus and the Greek text of the *Historia Monachorum*. Some are differences of phraseology, and these, while interesting and illuminating about Rufinus as a translator, have not been translated here. The major additions are given in translation. The more closely these are studied, the more clear it is that Rufinus is expanding and dealing in his usual free manner with the earlier Greek text. Considerable material is added to the chapter on John of Lycopolis, mostly in the form of a sermon on pride, which contains some interesting teaching on prayer and the monastic life; this has caused problems for the translator, since Rufinus uses terms which later became technical but which are here used in a less precise sense. There is also a long passage on Nitria and Scetis, perhaps taken from Rufinus's reminiscences of his own visit to Nitria, which provides essential material for the study of these monastic sites. Other additions are taken from other Macarian sources. The version of the passage on Evagrius given by Rufinus is a considerable improvement upon the Greek version, as it is that of John of Diolcos. Rufinus has used several New Testament quotations and also some quotations from the psalms which seem to be verbal reminiscences rather than direct quotation from a written source, and they have been translated accordingly.

The reference to the translation of the Greek text is given first by chapter and section, followed by the column number of the *PL* 21 text of Rufinus.

PROLOGUE

Prologue 4. This section is replaced by the following (cols 389–90):
Therefore at the beginning of my account, let us pray that the grace of our Lord Jesus Christ may be with us, for it is by his power that all the good works of the Egyptian monks have been performed. For we saw among them many fathers who while still on earth lived the life of heaven and new prophets who had such spiritual power that they held the office of seers, in testimony of whose merits the performance of signs and wonders was deservedly not lacking. For why should they, who covet nothing on earth nor of the flesh, not receive the power of heaven? We saw some who have put so far from them any thought of suspicion of evil that they have forgotten that there is evil in the world.

I JOHN OF LYCOPOLIS

I 1. The following is interpolated into the Greek text (col. 391):
Let us then take John first, as the true foundation of our work, and an example of every virtue, for he alone suffices and more than suffices to encourage pious and devout minds to attain the peak of virtue and to arouse them to attain the height of perfection.

We saw him in the district of the Thebaid in the desert which adjoins the city of Lyco living on a rock on a steep mountain. The path up to him was difficult and the approach to his hermitage was blocked and barricaded, so that from his fortieth to his ninetieth year—his age when we visited him— no-one had entered his hermitage. To those who came to him he let himself be seen at the window and from there he either gave them a word of God for edification or, if encouragement were needed, his answer. No woman, however, had been there, not even within his field of vision; even men he only saw rarely and at certain times. He had sensibly permitted an external cell to be built for guests in which those who had travelled from a distance could rest for a while. He, however, remained alone within, alone with God, never ceasing by day or night to pray and commune with God, striving with total purity of heart for the things of God and that which is beyond anything that can be thought. The more he separated himself from human cares and contacts, the nearer and closer was God to him. In short, he kept advancing in such sincerity of heart that he not only received from God a knowledge of those things which belong to the present time but was in fact deemed worthy of foreknowledge of those things that belong to the future. For God had clearly bestowed on him the gift of prophecy so that he predicted the future not only for people of his own city and province but often foretold events for the Emperor Theodosius, telling him which armies he would defeat in war, or in what way he would win a victory over the tyrants, or how many invasions by the barbarians he would have to endure.

I 2. The story of the general is as follows (col. 392):
Moreover, once when the Ethiopians had fallen upon a Roman army in the district of Cyrene (sic) which is the first city in the Thebaid from the direc- tion in which the Ethiopian lands lie, and had carried out several massacres of our men and carried off booty, the Roman *dux* came to see him. He was afraid to engage them because his force was very small while the enemy opposing him was a vast multitude. But John, designating a particular day, said, 'Go forward safely on the day I have named and you will defeat the enemy, capture spoils, and recover booty.' When what he had predicted

came to pass, he was loved and welcomed even by the emperor. But John believed that he had this grace of clairvoyance for the sake of those who asked questions rather than because of his own merits. For he used to say that these things were foretold by the Lord not for himself but for those who heard them.

I 3. This section is omitted in Rufinus.

I 4–9. The story of the tribune is replaced by the following (cols 392–3):
The Lord also showed another mighty wonder through him. A tribune going to take up his military command came to him and begged him to let his wife visit him; for, he said, she would endure many dangers for this end, as many as were necessary in order to see his face. At that time he would never make it his custom to see women, especially after he had enclosed himself in the hermitage on that cliff. The tribune persisted in his request and asserted that unless she saw him there was no doubt that she would perish simply from misery. When he had begged for this same thing over and over again and kept saying John would be the cause of his wife's death, so that from the place where she had hoped for salvation she would receive perdition, the old man, having regard as much to her faith as to her importunity, said, 'Go, your wife shall see me tonight: she shall not come here, but remain at home in bed.' After this, the man went home turning over this ambiguous reply in his mind. When he told his wife all about it, she was no less confused by the obscurity of the meaning of the message. When the time came to go to sleep, however, the man of God appeared to her in a vision and standing by the woman said, 'Your faith is great, woman, and so I have come to satisfy your desire: but I beg you not to go on wanting to see the face of the servants of God in reality, but rather to look upon their deeds and achievements with the spirit. For "it is the Spirit that quickens; the flesh profits nothing". (John 6.63) I am not a righteous man or a prophet as you suppose, but I have interceded for you to the Lord, because of your faith, and he has granted you healing of all those ills to which your body is exposed. Henceforth, both you and your husband will enjoy good health and all your household will be blessed. But you must be mind﹣ ful of the blessing the Lord has bestowed upon you and always fear God and ask no more than is due to you as your reward. Let this suffice, that you have seen me in sleep and do not ask for anything more.' When she woke up, the woman told her husband what she had seen and heard, describing the dress and the appearance of the man and all his distinguishing features. Her husband was amazed at this and going back to the man of God, he

gave thanks to God. He received a blessing from him and went away in peace.

I 11. This section is replaced by the following (col. 393):
Moreover, when many came to him, whether from his own district or from outside, he knew what they were coming for beforehand and revealed the hidden things of their hearts; if perchance some sin had been hidden he would seize upon it and denounce it in private and elicit both repentance and amendment. He also predicted the flooding of the Nile, saying whether there would be an abundance of water or a dearth. If perhaps some punish-ment or chastisement were threatened by God on human sins, he foretold it and showed what was the cause for which this catastrophe was looming.

I 12. This section is replaced by the following (col. 393):
He conferred healing and cures of the body on those who asked for them, but he shunned all publicity about this, and did not allow those who were afflicted to be brought to him, but blessed oil and gave it to them; and when they had been anointed with it, they were healed from whatever infirmity had afflicted them.

I 22–8. In place of this discourse Rufinus interpolates the following sermon (cols 395–8):
'The vice of arrogance is a serious one and most dangerous and overthrows even souls at the height of perfection; therefore I want you above all to beware of this. There is a species of this evil which is two-fold. It happens to some that in the first stages of their conversion, when either they have performed some small act of abstinence, or spent some money piously on the poor, then, just when they ought to take care to reject any such feeling, they behave as if they were superior to those on whom they have bestowed some-thing. There is, however, another kind of arrogance, when anyone who is approaching the highest virtue does not ascribe it wholly to God but to his own labours and zeal, and both seeks glory from men and loses it from God. Therefore, my little children, let us flee the vice of arrogance in any form, lest we fall into the trap the devil has put in our way.

'We must take great care also over our feelings and our thoughts. We must be careful that no greed, or depraved desire, or empty longing, or anything that is not of God, put its roots down in our hearts. From such roots vain and unhelpful thoughts spring up rapidly and continuously and cause us much distress, nor do they cease when we are praying; they are not put to shame when we stand in the presence of God and pray for our salvation, but they take our attention captive and when we seem to be standing in prayer in the body we are wandering about in attention and thought and are distracted by various things. Therefore, if there is anyone who thinks that he has renounced the world and the works of the devil, it is not enough to have renounced with the lips the possessions and lands and the affairs of this world; he must also renounce his own vices and profitless and empty pleasures. These are the things the Apostle is speaking about: "senseless and harmful desires that plunge men into their own destruction".' (1 Tim. 6.9)

'This therefore is what it means to renounce the devil and all his works. For through any sinful act or the onset of a perverse desire the devil enters into our hearts, for vices are from him just as virtues are from God. So if there are vices in our heart, when their prince the devil comes they give him room as their own creator and they introduce him to his own possessions. When this happens, such hearts can never have peace or stillness but are always thrown into disorder and held fast and oppressed, sometimes by an empty cheerfulness, sometimes by a vain sadness. For they have an evil occupant within them to whom they have given the means of entry through their passions and vices. On the other hand, a mind that has truly renounced the world, that is, one which has cut off and severed itself from every vice and has left the devil no means of entry, a mind which has checked anger, put down fury, avoided deceit, banished envy, and not only does not disparage its neighbour but does not even allow itself to think or suspect any evil of another and which takes to itself the joys of a brother and reckons his sadness as its own, a mind which observes these things and those like them opens itself to the Holy Spirit and, when he has entered and illuminated it, there will always grow therein the fruits of the Spirit which are joy, happiness, love, patience, long-suffering and goodness. This is what the Lord said in the Gospel: "A good tree cannot bear bad fruit, neither can a bad tree bear good fruit." (Matt. 7.18) For a tree is known by its fruit.

'There are some who seem to have renounced this age but have no concern for purity of heart, nor do they take care to cut the vices and passions out of their souls and build up character. They only take pains to see certain of the fathers and listen to some words from them which they can relate to others, in order to glorify themselves by having heard this or that father; and if by sheer chance either by listening or learning they discover a little knowledge, at once they want to become teachers and to teach not that which they have experienced but that which they have heard or seen, and they look down on others. They have a fondness for the clergy and they try to join them, not realising that it is a smaller condemnation if anyone who is strong in virtue does not dare to teach others than for someone who is ruled by passions and vices to teach others about virtue. So, my little children, I tell you that every kind of priesthood or sacerdotalism must be avoided, nor is it to be coveted in any way at all, but you must give yourselves up to the work of casting your vices from you and acquiring virtues of the soul. For it is left to the decision of God to call whom he wills and and when he wills to the ministry or priesthood. For "it is not the man who commends himself, but whom the Lord commends that is approved." (2 Cor. 10.18)

'The first work of a monk is to offer pure prayer to God with nothing reprehensible on his conscience. As the Lord says in the Gospel, "If you stand up to pray and remember that your brother has anything against you, unless you forgive your brother from your heart, neither will your Father which is in heaven forgive you." (Matt. 6.15) Then if, as we said before, we stand before God with a pure heart and free from all the passions and vices we have mentioned, we can, insofar as this is possible, see even God, and as we pray the eyes of our heart are turned towards him and we see that which is invisible with the spirit not with the flesh: this is a learning of the mind, and not a part of the flesh. For no one can suppose that he can behold the being of God in itself, but he shapes for himself some kind of appearance or image in his heart in some corporeal likeness. No form can be known in God, no limitations, but the understanding and the mind which is able to have understanding, and touch the love of the mind, can describe or relate, though it cannot comprehend. And so it behoves us to go towards God with all reverence and fear and thus set free in him the intuitions of the mind, that we may know him to be above whatever there is that the human mind can conceive that is splendid, clear, bright and majestic; and I say this, provided that there is purity of mind, totally freed of voluntary stains of sin.

'Those who have renounced the world and are seen to follow God must make this their central occupation; as the Scriptures say, "Be still and know that I am God". (Ps. 46.10) If then he will know God, insofar as that is possible for man, then at last he will understand everything else, he will know the mysteries of God, and insofar as his mind becomes more pure, so far will God reveal to him his secrets. He will become the friend of God, like those to whom the Saviour said, "I no longer call you servants but friends," (John 15.15) and whatever he asks, God will grant it to him, as to a dear friend. How greatly do the angelic virtues and all the mysteries of God love the friend of God and answer his petitions. And it is he whom neither death, nor life, nor angels, nor principalities, nor powers, nor any other creature can separate from the love of God which is in Christ Jesus. (cf. Rom. 8.39)

'And so, my beloved, seeing that you have chosen to please God and continue in his love, work hard to cast out whatever is alien to that end, all vices from the soul, all lusts from the body. The lusts of the body are not only vile sins which worldly men also reject, but we believe that in order to abstain from lusts whatever one seizes upon with greed is wrong, and there-fore we make use of abstinence. Even water and bread if they are eaten with greed, that is, not as being necessary for the body but to satisfy the inner desires, even this abstinence leads to the vice of lust. So it is our custom always to be careful of the vices of the inner man: The Lord wills to teach the soul to resist desires and longings when he says, "Enter in by the strait gate, for wide and spacious is the way which leads to death". (Matt. 7.13) for narrow and hard is the way that leads to life. The way is wide to the soul when it satisfies its desires in any way; it is narrow when it renounces its lusts. For this reason it is very profitable to seek a more secluded place in which to live and a solitary life, because in meeting with the brethren and in frequently coming and going the bridle of abstinence and poverty is relaxed, and by such happenings little by little one becomes accustomed to the use of things that are desirable, and even the most perfect of men can be taken prisoner by those. As David tells us, "I have fled far away and I remain in the wilderness; I am waiting for him who is able to save me from the raging wind and the tempest".' (Psalm 55.6,8)

XIII JOHN

XIII 7–8. In place of these two sections the following is interpolated (col. 434):
This man, moreover, continued steadfastly with the work he had begun and persevered tenaciously with his prayer. Indeed his feet split from his standing motionless for such a long time, so that a septic discharge flowed from them.

After he had completed three years there an angel of the Lord was sent and said to him, 'The Lord Jesus Christ and the Holy Spirit have received your prayers and healed the wounds of your body, and the bread of heaven, that is his word and wisdom, he gives you abundantly'. Then touching his mouth and feet, he restored his wounds to health and, full of grace and wisdom, he no longer felt the need for food. The angel ordered him to go to another place and to visit the surrounding hermitages and edify the brothers by the word and teaching of the Lord.

On Sundays he always returned to the same place for the grace of the sacrament and for the rest of his days he worked with his hands and wove from palm leaves harnesses for animals, as is the local custom.

XX 5–8. These sections are replaced by the following (cols 443–4):
Then we came to Nitria, the best-known of all the monasteries of Egypt, about forty miles from Alexandria; it takes its name from a nearby town where nitre is collected, having such a name, I believe, because the provid-ence of God foresaw that in these parts the sins of men would be washed away and obliterated just as stains are cleansed by nitre. In this place there are about fifty dwellings, or not many less, set near together and under one father. In some of them, there are many living together, in others a few and in some there are brothers who live alone. Though they are divided by their dwellings they remain bound together and inseperable in faith and love. So as we drew near to that place and they realised that foreign brethren were arriv-ing, they poured out of their cells like a swarm of bees and ran to meet us with delight and alacrity, many of them carrying containers of water and of bread, according to the rebuke of the prophet when he said to some, 'Ye came not forth to meet the children of Israel with bread and water'. (Neh. 13.2)When they had welcomed us, first of all they led us with psalms into the church and washed our feet and one by one they dried them with the linen cloth where-with they were girded, as if to wash away the fatigue of the journey, but in fact to purge away the hardships of worldly life with this traditional mystery.

What can I say that would do justice to their humanity, their courtesy, and their love; each of them wanted to take us to his own cell, not only to fulfil the duties of hospitality but even more out of humility, in which they are indeed masters, and out of gentleness and similar qualities which are learned among them according to graces that differ but with the one and same teaching, as if they had left the world for this one end. Nowhere have I seen love flourish so greatly, nowhere such quick compassion, such eager hospitality. And nowhere have I seen such meditation upon Holy Scripture, or a better understanding of it, or such discipline of sacred learning. You might well think that each of them was an expert in the wisdom of God.

XX 8. Rufinus's chapter on Cellia is interpolated after the sections on Nitria (cols 444–5):
Beyond this there is another place, the inner desert, about ten miles away. This is called Cellia because of the number of cells there, scattered about the desert. Those who have already begun their training there (i.e. in Nitria) and want to live a more remote life, stripped of external things, withdraw there. For this is the utter desert and the cells are divided from one another

by so great a distance that no-one can see his neighbour nor can any voice be heard. They live alone in their cells and there is a huge silence and a great quiet there. Only on Saturday and Sunday do they meet in church and then they see each other face to face as men restored to heaven. If it happens that anyone is missing from this gathering, they realise at once that he has been kept away by some indisposition of the body and they all go to visit him, not all together but at different times; each takes with him whatever he has that might be useful for the sick. But for no other reason does anyone dare to disturb the silence of his neighbour, unless it is to strengthen him with a word, as it might be to anoint with the strength of advice the athletes preparing for the contest. Many of them go three or four miles to the church and the distance between one cell and the next is no less, but so great is the love between them and so strong the affection by which they are bound to one another and towards all the brethren, that they are an example and a wonder to all. If anyone happens to want to live among them, as soon as they are aware of it, each of them offers him his own cell.

XX 9. The sections on Ammonius are preceded by the following interpolation (cols 445–6):
We saw a certain venerable father there, called Ammonius, a man in whom God had gathered together all his graces. When you saw how much charity he had, you would think you had never seen anything like it. If you considered his humility, you would think him more powerful in this than in anything else. But if you thought about his patience, or his gentleness or his kindness, you would think he excelled in each of these virtues and you would not know which came first. The gift of wisdom and learning was given him by God so abundantly that you would suppose none of the fathers to have gone so far into all the ways of knowledge. All that saw him said that no-one else had ever been so deeply drawn into the inner courts of the wisdom of God.

Also there were his two brothers, Eusebius and Euthymius, while Dioscorus, who was senior to him, had already been raised to the episcopate. These were brothers not only according to the flesh but were kin in their way of life, their practices and in all the virtues of their souls. As for all those brethren who lived in that place, they nourished them as a nurse with her children, strengthening them with teaching, and by their words leading them to shine at the height of perfection.

XX 14. This section is omitted and replaced by the following chapter on Origenes, who is not mentioned in the Greek text (col. 448):

There was also another monk who had been a disciple of Antony, Origines by name, a man magnificent in all things and of the highest prudence, who edified all who heard him by his words and descriptions of the virtues of his great master, and he enkindled them so much that you might have thought that they saw with their own eyes that of which he was speaking.

XX 15. The section of Evagrius is omitted and replaced by the following chapter (448–9):

We also saw a most learned man, wonderful in every way, Evagrius by name. To him among other powers of the soul was granted such grace in the discernment of spirits and the purging of thoughts (as the Apostle says) that it was thought that no other brother had ever achieved such subtle and spiritual knowledge. He had gathered his great understanding by his studies and his experience but above all by the grace of God. He was often instructed by Saint Macarius, who was known to all for his outstanding signs and miracles. Evagrius was unbelievably abstinent and above all he used to warn the brothers that if any of them pursued studies, whether for the humbling of the body or to repel fantasies of the demons, they should not drink a great deal of water. 'For,' he said, 'if the body is filled with water, it generates many fantasies and prepares a larger dwelling place for the demons.' He taught many other things about abstinence which he had gathered together deliberately. Not only did he use water very sparingly but he abstained entirely from bread. There were other brethren living in that place who confined themselves to bread and salt only, and in all that multitude of brothers there was scarcely one to be found who used oil at all. Many of them never lay down to sleep but sat and, as I have said, they were overtaken by sleep while they were meditating on the word of God.

XXI MACARIUS

The entire Greek chapter on Macarius the Egyptian is omitted and replaced by the following on the two Macarii (cols 449–52):

They told us also about two fathers who had lived there, the two Macarii, like twin lights illuminating the heavens, of whom one was an Egyptian by birth and had been a disciple of blessed Antony, the other an Alexandrian. As their names suggest, the virtues of their souls and the grace of heaven were in them marvellously combined. The one Macarius was equal to the other in feats of abstinence and in virtue of soul, and only excelled the other in that he possessed, as if inherited, the graces and powers of blessed Antony. They were both there when someone in the district committed the crime of murder and someone else who was innocent was charged with the crime. He who suffered this calumny fled to their cell and those who pursued him came too, alleging that they were in danger unless they handed over the man accused of murder to the law. On the other hand he protested that he was innocent of this crime, and affirmed by an oath that he was not guilty of blood. At last since both sides were unshakable, Saint Macarius asked them where the man who had been killed was buried. They pointed out the place and he went to the tomb with the man and all those who accused him. There he knelt down and called upon the name of Christ, and said to those who stood nearby, 'Now the Lord will show if indeed the man is guilty whom you accuse.' Raising his voice he called the dead by name and he who was called replied from the grave. Macarius said to him, 'By the grace of Christ, I ask you to say if this man who is accused here is the one who killed you'. Then he replied in a clear voice from the grave, saying that this was not the man by whom he had been killed. Stupefied they all fell to the ground and they begged him, grovelling at his feet, to ask the dead man who had killed him. 'This,' he said, 'I will not ask; it is enough for me to have set the innocent free; it is not up to me to discover the guilty.'

The story of the cure of the girl who thought she was a mare (XXI 17) is told at this point (col. 451) but with a significant difference: where the Greek suggests that it was her delusion, the Latin says, 'She seemed to men to have been turned into a horse, and they thought she was a horse not a girl.'

Rufinus continues:
Another story is about a little girl who was brought to him, her body so diseased in all its parts that the flesh was eaten away and the inside parts were laid bare, and there an innumerable host of worms was breeding, so that no one was able to come near her because of the horror of the stench. She was brought to him by her parents and thrown down in front of his door; he had pity on the tormented girl and said, 'Be calm, my daughter, for the Lord has given you this for salvation and not for death. It is a great work of providence so that you should not be in danger.' When he had arranged for prayers to be said for seven days continuously, he blessed oil and anointed her limbs in the name of the Lord and so he restored her health, but in such a way that no femininity showed in her form, no female parts were apparent, so that in all her contact with men, she never beguiled them with womanly deceits.

They said that once a heretic came to him with that heresy which is found in Egypt. When he had spoken with much art to the brethren who lived in the desert whom he disturbed, he dared to assert his depraved beliefs even before Macarius. When the old man had argued with him, and contra-dicted him, he eluded the simple words with clever arguments. When the saint saw that the faith of the brothers was in danger, he said, 'What a thing it is, that our arguments should subvert the hearers. Let us go to the grave of a brother who has gone before us in the Lord, and let us pray to God to raise the dead man from his grave so that all may know whose faith is approved by God.' This word pleased all the listeners and they went to the grave. Macarius urged the heretic to call upon the name of the Lord, but he said, 'Sir, it was your idea, you call first'. So Macarius postrated himself and when he had prayed enough he raised his eyes to heaven and said to the Lord, 'Lord, show which of the two of us has the true faith by raising this dead man.' And when he had said this, they called the name of the dead brother who was buried there. He who was in the grave replied at once and the brothers hastened and took down the front of the tomb and let him come out, trailing the remains of the grave-clothes in which he had been wrapped, and he appeared alive. When the heretic saw this he was astonished and fled. All the brethren followed him and cast him out beyond their borders.

Many more things were said of him, which are too numerous to be written down; but these few have been selected from many so that the rest of his works may be surmised.

XXIII MACARIUS OF ALEXANDRIA

XXIII 1. This section is omitted and replaced by the following interpolation (cols 452–5):
Another Saint Macarius has also attained splendid virtues; others have also written some things about them which should suffice to enable one to get an idea of the greatness of his virtues, and so we shall omit them for the sake of brevity.

They said, however, that he was a lover more than anyone else of the desert and that he had explored its ultimate and inaccessible wastes. . . .
There follows a variant of the Jannes and Jambres story, assigned in the Greek text to Macarius the Egyptian (XXI 5–8).

Rufinus continues (col. 453):
The place where Saint Macarius lived is called Scetis. It is in a great valley, a day and a night's journey from the monasteries of Nitria, and the way to

it is not found or shown by any track or landmarks on the ground, but one journeys by the signs and courses of the stars. Water is hard to find, and when it is found it has a bad smell, bituminous, yet inoffensive to the taste. Here men are made perfect in holiness, for none but those of austere resolution and supreme constancy can endure such a terrible spot. But their chief concern is the love they show one another and those who happen to arrive there.

One day someone gave Saint Macarius a bunch of grapes, and he, thinking not of himself but others (1 Cor. 13.5) sent them to another brother whom he thought was more delicate than himself. Then the recipient gave thanks to God for his brother's gift, but he likewise did not think of himself but of others and sent them to someone else, and this one to the next, and thus they passed through all the cells which are scattered about in the desert far from each other, each recipient ignorant of the original sender; at last they were returned to him who had first sent them away, Saint Macarius marvelled to see in the brethren such self-control and such brotherly love and he continued with more vigour his own attempts at the life of the spirit.

To confirm our faith we were told this by those who had heard it from his own lips: one night a demon came and knocked on the door of his cell and said, 'Get up, Macarius, and go to the meeting, where the brethren have met to celebrate vigils.' But he, filled with the grace of God, could not be deceived, and he recognised a lie of the devil and said, 'You liar and enemy of the truth, what do you know about the meeting, when we are gathered together with the saints?' Then the demon replied, 'Don't you know, Macarius, that without us there is never any meeting or gathering of monks?' Macarius replied, 'The Lord is in control of you, unclean demon'. And turning to prayer, he asked the Lord to show him if the boast of the demon was true. Then he went to the meeting where the brothers had met to celebrate vigils, and again he prayed to the Lord to show him if this statement had been true. And behold he saw the whole church as it were filled with little black Ethiopian boys, running hither and thither and doing whatever they wanted to do. The brothers conducted themselves as usual, all being seated while one of them repeated a psalm and the rest either listened or made the responses. The Ethiopian boys ran among them, teasing each of those sitting down, and if they could put two fingers over their eyes they sent them to sleep at once. If they could put their fingers into their mouths, they made them yawn. After the psalm when the brothers prostrated themselves in prayer they ran to each of them, and as each threw himself forward to pray they assumed the appearance of women, while others made themselves into things to eat or drink, or did other things. And whenever the demons formed themselves into something as if in mockery, distractions entered the minds of those praying; and yet there were some who when the demons began to do something to them, repelled them as if by force and threw themselves forward so that they did not dare to stand in front of them or come alongside them, while they were able to play on the heads or the backs of the weaker brethren who were not intent on their prayers. When Saint Macarius saw this, he groaned heavily, and weeping freely he said to the Lord, 'Behold, O Lord and do not keep silence, neither be gentle, O God.' (Ps. 83.1) 'Arise and let your enemies be scattered and let them flee before your face; for our souls are filled with illusions.' (Ps. 68.1) After the prayers he called each of the brothers to him, to find out the truth, and before whichever face he had seen the demons playing in diverse ways and various images, he asked them if while they were praying or collecting their thoughts they had wandered away or followed any of the things which he had seen them imagining through the demons. And each confessed to him what had been in his mind as he urged them. And then he understood that all vain and superfluous thoughts that anyone conceived during either the psalms or the prayers came from the illusions of the demons. Those who were able to keep control of their hearts were able to resist the black Ethiopians. He who joins his heart to God and remains intent at the time of prayer, can receive into himself nothing that is alien or superfluous.

He said that something much worse was seen at that time, when the brethren approached the sacrament. When they stretched out their hands to receive it, Ethiopians came first to some of their hands and placed coal there, and the Host which the priest seemed to be bringing in his hands returned to the altar. There were others, however, who rejoiced in greater goodness and when they extended their hands to the altar the demons drew back and fled away afraid. Then he saw the angel of the Lord coming to their aid and placing his hands over the hands of the priest while he was distributing the sacrament. From that time on, he was permitted by the grace of God that whenever at vigils during the psalms and prayers any brother entertained in his heart the illusions of the demons, he would know of it, and when they came to the altar neither their unworthiness nor their merits would be concealed.

XXIII 4. After the story of the two Macarii on the ferry Rufinus concludes the chapter with the following sentence (col. 455):
But, as I have said, many more wonderful things are related concerning the deeds of Macarius the Alexandrian, some of which you can find in the eleventh book of my *Ecclesiastical History.*

XXIV PAUL

XXIV 7. The following is interpolated (col. 458):
One day when some of the brethren had come to Antony, and they were great and perfect men, it happened that Paul was present with them. And when they had discoursed on profound and mystical matters in which they frequently referred to the prophets and to the Saviour, Paul asked, in the simplicity of his heart, whether Christ came first or the prophets. Blessed Antony found what he had asked absurd, and blushed to find him more simple than usual, and he told him to keep quiet and go away. Because Paul had been told that whatever was said to him was an order in the service of God, he went to his cell as if he had received an order and began to be quiet, not speaking to anyone. When Antony saw this, he began to wonder that Paul should take pleasure in behaving like that, for he did not realise what he had said to him. So he ordered him to speak and tell him why he was keeping quiet and Paul said to him, 'Father, you told me yourself to go away and keep quiet'. Antony was astounded that he had taken such notice of his words when he had pronounced them casually. 'He condemns us all,' he said 'When we were not listening to what we were saying about heaven, he carried out whatever words came out of our mouth.'

XXVI JOHN

Rufinus omits this chapter and replaces it by the following (col. 460):
There was in that place a holy man, entirely filled with the gift of grace, called John; in him so great was the gift of consolation that whoever came to him with any grief or oppression of spirit, after a few words with him they would go away filled with zeal and joy. Many graces of healing were given him from the Lord.

THE SYRIAC VERSION

GREEK	SYRIAC	GREEK	SYRIAC
Prologue	1 Prologue	20 Dioscorus	Dioscorus
1 John of Lycopolis	2 John of Lycopolis		16 Copres Patermuthius
2 Or	3 Or		17 Sourous ('Or')
3 Ammon	4 Ammon		18 Evagrius
4 Bes	5 Bes		19 Pityrion
5 Oxyrhynchus	6 Oxyrhynchus		20 Epilogue
6 Theon	7 Theon	Nitria	21 Nitria
7 Elias	8 Elias		22 Amoun
8 Apollo	9 Apollo	(Ammonius)	23 Ammonius
9 Amoun	Amoun	(Didymus)	24 Didymus
10 Copres Patermuthius		(Cronides)	25 Cronides
11 Sourous		(The 3 brothers)	26 The 3 brothers
12 Helle	10 Helle ('Apelles')	(Evagrius)	
		21 Macarius	
13 Apelles	11 Apelles ('Apollo')	22 Amoun	
		23 Macarius of Alexandria	
John	John	24 Paul	
14 Paphnutius	12 Paphnutius	25 Piammonas	27 Piammonas ('Philemon')
15 Pityrion			
16 Eulogius	13 Eulogius	26 John	28 John
17 Isidore	14 Isidore		29 Sarapion
18 Sarapion			30 Apollonius
19 Apollonius		Epilogue	

A COMPARATIVE TABLE OF CHAPTERS OF THE GREEK AND
SYRIAC VERSIONS OF THE HISTORIA MONACHORUM

THE SYRIAC VERSION

A Syriac version of the *Historia Monachorum* has come down to us in Anani-sho's *Paradise of the Holy Fathers*. This work is a Syriac recension of the *Life of St Antony*, the *Lausiac History*, the *Rule of Pachomius*, the *Historia Monachorum* and a collection of Apophthegmata; it was meant to be the Syrian monk's complete guide to the Egyptian Fathers. The text was first published by P. Bedjan, *Acta Martyrum et Sanctorum* VII (Leipzig-Paris 1890). The Syriac with an English translation by E. Wallis Budge was printed privately in 1904. Budge's English translation was issued separately in 1907 in two volumes entitled *The Paradise of the Holy Fathers*. There is a brief discussion of Ananisho's text in Butler's *Lausiac History* (vol. 1, pp. 77–96, 266–7) but much more authoritative now is R. Draguet's introduc-tion to his *Les formes syriaques de la matière de l'histoire lausiaque* (4 vols, 2 Syriac and 2 French translation), *Corpus Scriptorum Christianorum Orien-talium, Scriptores Syri* 169–70, 173–4 (1978).

Ananisho was a Nestorian monk of the Monastery of Beth Abhe near Nisibis in Mesopotamia who lived in the seventh century. Thomas of Marga (fl. 840) tells us in the *Book of the Governors* (Bk II, ch. XI) that in prepara-tion for his work Ananisho visited Scetis, 'where he learned concerning all the manner of the lives of the ascetic fathers, whose histories and questions are written in books, and concerning their dwellings, and the places in which they lived'.

The *Historia Monachorum* is attributed by Ananisho to St Jerome. The first nine chapters follow the Greek order, but after that the list is seriously disrupted, and the two Macarii and Paul the Simple are omitted altogether. The Syriac translation, however, appears to follow the Greek original very literally. Indeed the minor variations from the readings of the critical text indicate clearly that the Greek manuscript underlying the Syriac version belonged to Festugière's **p** family. But only the major interpolations are given here in Budge's translation (lightly adapted).[1] The Greek references are given first by chapter and section followed by the page number in vol. 1 of *The Paradise of the Holy Fathers*.

1. Thanks are due to Chatto and Windus Ltd for permission to use copyright material from E. Wallis Budge, *The Paradise of the Holy Fathers*. We should also like to thank Dr Sebastian Brock for his help with information on Ananisho.

I JOHN OF LYCOPOLIS

I 63. The Syriac omits this section on the contemplative life and interpolates the following (p. 333):

But the spectator of the mind who leaves all these things for others to administer [or provide] is far better, and more excellent and greater than he, and he pursues spiritual instead of corporeal things, and leaves the transitory things of this world to others; for he denies himself and forgets himself, and takes up his cross and cleaves to Christ, and embraces the things of heaven continually, and he makes his escape from everything [earthly] and draws near to God, and he will not allow himself to be drawn to turn behind him through any care whatsoever. And such a man as this is, through his godly works and the praises which he offers up continually before God, with God, and, being free and unfettered by any ties whatsoever, he stands before God in security, and his mind is not drawn away by any other care. He who is in this condition holds converse with God continually, and offers up to him unceasing praise and glory. But it is necessary [that those who seek after God should forsake] everything which is visible, and should turn themselves completely towards God, and should commit themselves to him that he may protect their lives; for the man in whom God dwells does not know even that the world exists, since the whole of creation is an alien things in his eyes, because he is crucified to all the world and it is accounted by him as nothing.

IV BES

IV 3. The Syriac omits the last sentence.

X PATERMUTHIUS

X 4. The Syriac interpolates (p. 365):

And being unable to go into her house and plunder it, because the roofs of the house were as flat as the ground and they had no rain water pipes [leading into it], for there is no rain in the Thebaid, and there was no place on the roof whereby he could enter the house, or by which he could leave it again, and he was neither able to descend nor to escape from it . . .

X 6. The Syriac interpolates (p. 365):

. . . departed into the desert. And when he had lived [there] for five weeks without bread, a man came to him carrying bread and water, and he entreated him to partake of it and refresh himself.

X 32. In the Syriac version the Manichaean is wholly consumed in the fire (p. 371).

XII HELLE

XII 16. The Syriac omits this section and places it at the end of the chapter on Copres and Patermuthius.

XIII JOHN

XIII 9. The Syriac precedes this section with the following interpolation (p. 357): Now a certain man who was paralysed wished to go to him and be healed, and immediately his legs touched the back of the ass which he was going to ride, through his faith only they were healed, before the holy man had offered up even a prayer on his behalf.

XVIII SARAPION

XVIII 3. The Syriac transfers the last sentence to the next chapter on Apollonius.

XIX APOLLONIUS

XIX 12. The Syriac omits this section and replaces it by the following (p. 382): And we ourselves saw the *martyrium* in which he and those who had testified with him were laid, and we prayed and worshipped God, and also touched their dead bodies, for they were not as yet buried because of the inundation of the Nile, but lay embalmed upon their biers in the Thebaid, and for this reason we made ready to insert here the history of the man.

XXII AMOUN

XXII 7–9. The Syriac omits these sections.

EPILOGUE

8. The Syriac assumes that Diolcos is on the bank of the Nile (p. 375).

BIBLIOGRAPHY
of primary and secondary selected sources

I. PRIMARY SOURCES

Aetheria, *Egeria's Travels,* trans. and notes by John Wilkinson, London, 1971.

Ammonas, *Letters of Ammonas,* English trans. Derwas Chitty, SLG Press, 1979.

Antony the Great, *The Letters of St Antony,* trans. Derwas Chitty, SLG Press, 1977.

Apophthegmata Patrum, Alphabetical Series, ed. *PG* 65, cols 71–440. English trans. Benedicta Ward *The Sayings of the Desert Fathers,* Mowbray, 1975. *Systematic Series,* partial translation Benedicta Ward, *Wisdom of the Desert Fathers,* SLG Press, 1979.

Athanasius, *Vita S. Antonii, PG* 26, cols 835–976. English trans. R. T. Meyer, ACW, London, 1950.

Basil St, *Opera Omnia,* ed. Garnier, Paris, 1721–30; *PG* 29–32.

Cassian, John, *Institutes,* ed. and trans. J.–C. Guy, *SC* 109. *Conferences,* ed. and trans. E. Pichery, *SC* 42, 54, 64.

Cyril of Scythopolis, *Vitae Euthymii, Sabae* etc., French trans. A.-J. Festugière in *Les Moines d'Orient* III, Paris, 1961–3.

Eusebius, *Historia Ecclesiastica,* ed. and trans. K. Lake, London, 1926.

Evagrius Ponticus, *Opera Omnia, PG* 40, cols 1213–86. English trans. of *Praktikos,* John Eudes Bamberger, Kalamazoo, 1967.

Jerome St, *Opera Omnia, PL* 22–30. Letters trans. C. C. Mierow, *The Letters of St Jerome,* ACW, London, 1963.

Pachomius, *Vita Prima,* ed. A.-J. Festugière, text and trans. in *Les Moines d'Orient,* Paris, 1965.

Palladius, *Lausiac History,* ed. C. Butler, Texts and Studies 6, Cambridge, vol. I, Prolegomena, 1898; vol. II, introduction and text, 1904. English trans. R. T. Meyer, *The Lausiac History,* ACW, London 1965.

Rufinus, *Historia Monachorum in Aegypto, PL* 21, cols 387–462.

Socrates, *Historia Ecclesiastica, PG* 67, cols 29–872, ed. Hussey, 3 vols, Oxford, 1853.

Sozomen, *Historia Ecclesiastica, PG* 67, cols 844–1630, ed. Hussey, Oxford, 1860.

Theodoret, *Historia Ecclesiastica*, ed. Gaisford, Oxford, 1954. *Histoire des Moines de Syrie* (1), ed. and trans. Pierre Canivet, *SC* 234, Paris, 1977.

2. SECONDARY SOURCES

Abel, F.‑M., *Géographie de la Palestine*, 2 vols, Paris, 1933, 1938.

Batiffol, P., *Études de liturgie et d'archaeologie chrétienne*, Paris, 1919.

Brown, Peter, *The World of Late Antiquity*, London, 1971. *The Making of Late Antiquity*, Harvard, 1978. 'The Rise and Function of the Holy Man in Late Antiquity', *Journal of Roman Studies* 61 (1971), 80–101.

Budge, E. Wallis, *The Wit and Wisdom of the Desert Fathers*, Oxford, 1934. *The Paradise of the Holy Fathers*, 2 vols, London, 1907.

Chadwick, Owen, *John Cassian*, Cambridge, 1950.

Chitty, Derwas, *The Desert a City*, Oxford, 1966.

Clarke, Somers, *Christian Antiquities of the Nile Valley*, Oxford, 1912.

de Cosson, A., *Mareotis*, London, 1938.

Dawes E. and Baynes N. H., *Three Byzantine Saints*, Oxford, 1948/1979.

Delehaye, H., *Les origines du culte des martyrs*, Brussels, 1912.

Devos, Paul, 'Les nombres dans l'Historia Monachorum in Aegypto,' *Anal. Boll.* 92 (1974), 97–108.

Draguet, R., 'L'Histoire Lausiaque, une oeuvre écrite dans l'esprit d'Évagre', *Révue d'Histoire ecclésiastique*, 1946, 321–364.

Evelyn White, H. G. *The Monasteries of the Wadi'n Natrun*: part 11, *The History of the Monasteries of Nitria and Scetis*, New York, 1932–7.

Festugière, A.‑J. *Les Moines d'Orient*: I. *Culture et Sainteté*, Paris, 1961. II. *Lives of Hypatius and Daniel the Stylite*, Paris, 1962. III. *Cyril of Scythopolis' Lives*, Paris, 1962–3. IV. *Historia Monachorum* and *Vita Prima of Pachomius*, Paris, 1965. (French translations with notes). The Greek text of the *Historia Monachorum*, *Subsidia Hagiographia* 34, Brussels, 1961. Reissued with French translation as No. 53, Brussels, 1971.

Frank, T., *An Economic History of Rome*, Baltimore, 1927.

Grabar, A., *Martyrium*, Paris, 1946.

Guillaumont, A., 'Les fouilles françaises des Kellia', see Wilson, R. McL., below.

Hardy, E. R., *Christian Egypt: Church and People* New York, 1931. *The Large Estates of Byzantine Egypt* Oxford, 1931.

Hausherr, I., *Penthos, Orientalia Christiana Analecta* 132, Rome 1942.

Jones, A. H. M., *The Later Roman Empire 284–602*, Oxford, 1964.

Kasser, R., 'Fouilles Suisses aux Kellia', see Wilson, R. McL., below.

Kelly, J., *Jerome, his Life, Writings, and Controversies*, London, 1975.

MacKean, W. H., *Christian Monasticism in Egypt to the Close of the Fourth Century*, London, 1920.

Merton, Thomas, *The Wisdom of the Desert*, London, 1960.

Murphy, F. K., *Rufinus of Aquileia (345–411): His Life and Works*, Washington, 1945.

Petrie, Sir W. M. F., *A History of Egypt:* vol. v, *Egypt under Roman Rule*, J. G. Milne, London, 1924.

Pitra, J., *Juris Ecclesiastici Graecorum, Historia et Monumenta*, 2 vols, Rome, 1864.

Preuschen, E., *Palladius und Rufinus: ein Beitrag zur Quellenkunde des ältesten Mönchtums*, Giessen, 1897.

Rostovtzeff, M., *Social and Economic History of the Roman Empire*, Oxford, 1926.

Rousseau, P., *Ascetics, Authority, and the Church in the age of Jerome and Cassian*, Oxford, 1978.

Telfer, W., 'The Trustworthiness of Palladius', *Journal of Theological Studies* 38 (1937), 379–83.

Thélamon, F., 'Modèles du monachisme oriental selon Rufin d'Aquilée,' *Anticlita Altoadriatiche* 12 (1977), 323–5.

Veilleux, A., *La liturgie dans le cénobitisme pachômien au quatrième siècle*, Studia Anselmiana 57, Rome, 1968.

Waddell, H., *The Desert Fathers*, London, 1936.

Ware, K., 'The Monk and the Married Christian: comparisons in early monastic sources', *Eastern Churches Revue* 7 (1974), 72–84.

Wilson, R. McL., *The Future of Coptic Studies*, Leiden, 1978.

CHRONOLOGICAL TABLE

c. 251   Antony born.

285   Antony withdraws to Pispir.

c. 292   Pachomius born.

c. 293   Macarius the Alexandrian born.

c. 300   Macarius the Egyptian born.

c. 305   Apollo born.

313   Antony withdraws to the Interior Mountain by the Red Sea.
Pachomius baptized.

c. 320   Pachomius founds community at Tabennisi.

328   Athanasius bishop of Alexandria.

330   Athanasius in the Thebaid.
Amoun moves to Nitria?
Macarius the Egyptian goes to Scetis?

333   Macarius the Alexandrian baptized.

338   Antony visits Alexandria and Nitria.
Foundation of Cellia.

340   Athanasius, Ammonius the Tall and Isidore in Rome; monastic
ideas spread in West.

346   Pachomius dies.

c. 350   John of Lycopolis enclosed.

355   Macarius the Alexandrian becomes a monk.

356   Antony dies.

357   Athanasius writes *Vita S. Antonii.*

361–3   Julian the Apostate emperor.

365

(or 373)   First civil edict concerning monks (Valens).

373   Athanasius dies.
Melania in Egypt.
Rufinus in Egypt, Nitria and Pispir.

379   Theodosius emperor in the East.

383   Evagrius in Nitria.

385   Jerome and Paula come to Egypt and visit Nitria.
      Apollo founds coenobium at Bawit.
      Evagrius at Cellia.
      Cassian and Germanus arrive in Egypt.

388   Palladius comes to Egypt; visits Alexandria, Nitria and Cellia.

c. 390   Macarius the Egyptian dies.

391–2   Destruction of Serapeum.

393   Dioscorus bishop of Hermopolis Parva (Damanhur).
      Macarius the Alexandrian dies.

394   Arsenius goes to Scetis?
      John of Lycopolis visited by Palladius and by the seven monks
         from Jerusalem.
      The journey narrated in *HM*.

395   John of Lycopolis dies.
      Theodosius dies.

399   Evagrius dies.
      Theophilus's Paschal Letter against Anthropomorphism.
      Cassian leaves Egypt.
      Theophilus turns against Origen.

400   Synod at Alexandria condemns Origenism.
      Tall brothers etc. exiled from Egypt.

403   Exiled monks return to their monasteries.

404   Jerome translates the *Pachomian Rule*.

c. 405   Writing of the *HM*.

405–10   Rufinus translates the *HM*.

407–8   First devastation of Scetis.

412   Cyril bishop of Alexandria.
      Palladius leaves Egypt.

419–20   Writing of the *Lausiac History*.

420–30   Cassian writes the *Institutes* and *Conferences*.

c. 440   Theodoret writes the *Philotheos Historia*.

INDEX OF PERSONS AND PLACES

(References to the Greek text are by chapter and section in bold type)

SUBJECT INDEX

(References to the Greek text are by chapter and section in bold type)